The
Noodle
Cook
Book

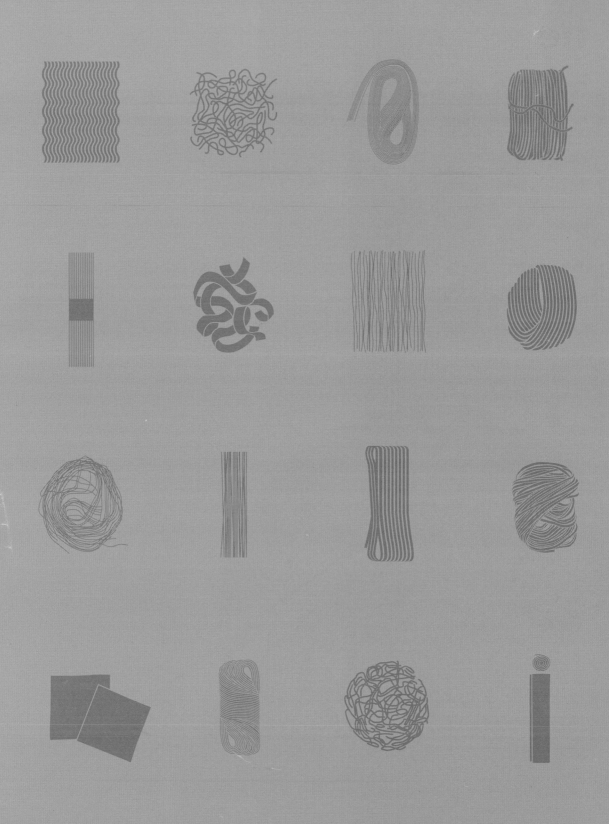

The

Noodle Cook Book

101 healthy and delicious noodle recipes for happy eating

EBURY PRESS

Noodlistas Unite!

When I was originally approached with the idea of putting together a cookbook, I knew that there would be far too many recipes that I love and too many regions that they originate from to all be included in a single book, so I decided to begin with my first passion, noodles, because that is what I also focused the company on.

For those who don't know my backstory, I began Mr Lee's Pure Foods Co., AKA Mr Lee's Noodles, due to a combination of necessity and frustration. I had been diagnosed with stage 4 cancer and was given very little advice for how to deal with it beyond the usual chemical and medicinal avenues that doctors make you travel. When it came to diet, I was given a long list of don'ts and unfortunately it included one of my favourite food groups, noodles.

Being of Singaporean and Australian heritage, I'd been raised on noodles my entire life, but when I started to dig into the ingredients of most modern noodle recipes, I found that I would have to either stop eating the noodle dishes that I love to have a stronger chance at survival, or I'd have to develop a 'no nasties' approach to the traditional dishes themselves.

I'm now a big believer of 'you are what you eat', so I decided to take a stand and as a result, Mr Lee's ethos of 'no nasties' healthier choices for time-poor people was born. An ethos that would allow me to enjoy the dishes that I love without the junk ingredients that we have all started to believe are necessary for all of those wonderful flavours. I initially fought the cancer that should have claimed me in 2014 and subsequently three more times since and simultaneously brought Mr Lee's Pure Foods Co. into the world.

For this book I decided along with my wonderful Mr Lee's Chef team, Andy Chu and Jackie Kearney, to separate the recipes into six chapters: Thai, Chinese, Japanese, Korean, Vietnamese, and Mr Lee's Asian Favourites. We have taken much-loved traditional dishes and given them the Mr Lee's makeover. Importantly most of us are also very time poor nowadays, so our recipes are all designed to be prepped and cooked in 30 minutes or less.

All too often you have to visit a specialist grocery store to source the ingredients for your favourite noodle dish and sometimes it is likely to be far from good for you, but in this book, we've taken great pains to make each dish as healthy as possible without compromising any of the flavour, but more importantly, we ensured that we spared you the trips to Chinatown or Koreatown and so on, that you would have had to have made in the past, because the ingredients in the following pages are able to be sourced at any of your major supermarkets.

But as I started by saying, this is just the beginning. At Mr Lee's, we're developing many other staples of the Oriental-Pan Asian diet in the same ethos; such as our congee range, so I hope to be able to bring you much more than noodles in the future. But for now – from myself and everyone at Mr Lee's, we hope you enjoy the recipes in this book and it helps you make healthier choices.

Stay positive, stay healthy!

Damien King Lee

I couldn't have done it without:
Andy Chu, Executive Chef; Jackie Kearney, Development Chef and Writer. Thanks too, Weronika Lee, Martin Flavin, James Roberts.

Andy Chu   Jackie Kearney   Damien King Lee

Mr Lee's Noodle Store Cupboard

Noodles are just noodles, right? Nah, think again. There are hundreds of different types. Fat, chewy ones; thin, delicate ones; wheat-based, rice-based, gluten free. Some are world famous; some are local legends. There are loads of options and it's worth having a few different types in your store cupboard. Some dried noodles will last for months, while fresh ones, like chow mein, ho fun or udon can be kept in your fridge, just waiting to bring some noodle-y goodness to your day. Now, even though some noodles work particularly well for certain recipes, there are no 'wrong' noodles to use. We're not going to come round and confiscate your wok. To make it easier, we've grouped the noodles to help you swap them around as you like.

If you are looking for vegan or gluten-free options, remember to check the ingredients list on the packaging to make sure you pick the right noodles for your dietary needs. It's worth remembering that many yellow and chow mein noodles often don't contain egg but are coloured yellow. Check the label if you are looking for either vegan yellow noodles or specifically egg noodles.

NAME	TYPE	ORIGIN
Dried egg noodle	Egg noodle	China
Chow mein (also known as Hong Kong noodle)	Egg or yellow noodle	Southern China
Fresh egg noodle (also known as Hokkien noodle)	Egg and wheat noodle	China
Dried or fresh wheat noodle	Wheat noodle	China
Shanghai noodle	Wheat noodle	Shanghai
Lo Mein noodle	Wheat and egg noodle	China

THE NOODLE COOKBOOK

DESCRIPTION	GREAT FOR	TASTE + TEXTURE
Pale yellow. Width ranges from thin to medium–thick. Available in most supermarkets.	Stir-fry/ Crispy noodles/ Soup	Toothsome and chewy.
Yellow dried medium–thick noodle. Available in most supermarkets.	Stir-fry/ Crispy noodles	
Available in supermarket fridges or vacuum-packed on shelves. You'll get better quality from an east Asian supermarket. Width ranges from thin to medium–thick.	Soup/ Lo mein/ Stir-fry	Soft texture, sometimes lightly oily (Hokkien-type). Need lightly blanching.
Generic, thin pale noodle, easy to find on most supermarket shelves. Also available as dried or fresh spinach noodle.	Soup/ Stir-fry/ Anything except chow mein	Soft texture, with a little bite.
Thicker than udon. Available in east Asian supermarket fridges or vacuum-packed on shelves.	Stir-fry only	Slightly oily, fresh, thick noodle with lots of bite.
Can be dried or fresh. Slightly yellow colour & thinner than chow mein or Hong Kong noodle. Widely available in larger Chinese supermarkets.	Stir-fry/ Soups/ Crispy noodles	Soft texture with a little bite, similar to ramen.

NAME	TYPE	ORIGIN
Udon noodle	Wheat noodle	Japan
Crispy e-fu noodle (also known as yi mein)	Wheat and egg noodle	China
Dan dan noodle	Wheat noodle	China
Ramen noodle	Wheat noodle	Japan
Jajang noodle (also known as jajangmyeon, chunjang or chajang)	Wheat noodle	Korea
Ho fun noodle (also known as sha ha fen)	Rice noodle (gluten-free)	China
Flat rice noodle	Rice noodle (gluten-free)	China/ South East Asia
Cheung fun noodle	Rice noodle, sometimes also made with tapioca starch (gluten-free)	China

DESCRIPTION	GREAT FOR	TASTE + TEXTURE
Thick, round noodle. Available in supermarket fridges or vacuum-packed on shelves. Better quality available from an east Asian supermarket. You can occasionally find dried versions.	Stir-fry/ Soup	Soft, smooth noodle with little bite – similar to Shanghai noodle.
Thick, large dried noodle cake, that cooks instantly after soaking. A large wok is needed to fit the size of the noodle cake. Available in east Asian supermarkets.	Often used for Chinese celebrations/ Stir-fry/ Soup	Soft and smooth, with a strong, creamy flavour of egg and oil.
Medium–thick noodle, available fresh or dried, usually shaped in a cake. Available in east Asian supermarkets, either fresh in fridges or dried on shelves.	Soup/ Lo mein	Soft with a little bite, similar to ramen noodles.
Medium noodle, available fresh or dried. Available in supermarket fridges or vacuum-packed on shelves. You'll get better quality from an east Asian supermarket.	Soup/ Stir-fry	Smooth texture and creamy taste. Good-quality fresh ramen noodles are similar to e-fu.
Pale yellow egg noodle with a white floury outside. Looks a little like short, slightly flattened spaghetti in the packet. Available in east Asian supermarkets – mostly dried, but occasionally frozen.	Stir-fry/ Soup	Thicker, chewy wheat noodle. Similar to dan dan.
Flat, thick fresh rice noodles. Can be frozen, but tastes best when eaten as fresh as possible. Available in east Asian supermarket fridges.	Stir-fry/ Soup	Smooth and slightly toothsome noodle. Similar to Thai noodle sen yai.
Available in varying widths.	Stir-fry/ Soup/ Stews	Bite depends on liquid and cooking time: in a soup, they are slippery and soft, in a stir-fry the noodles have more bite.
Rice-based noodle is made from rolled rice noodle sheets, and often cut into bite-sized pieces. Found in Chinese supermarket fridges.	Steam/ Pan-fry/ Stir-fry	Smooth but firm-bodied texture with a nice bite. Absorbs flavour.

NAME	TYPE	ORIGIN
Dried rice vermicelli	Rice noodle (gluten-free)	China/ South East Asia
Fresh rice vermicelli	Rice noodle	China/ South East Asia
Fine rice vermicelli Sheets (also known as rice noodle cakes or sheets)	Rice noodle (gluten-free)	Vietnam/ Korea
Sen yai noodle (also known as fresh Thai rice noodle)	Rice noodle with tapioca starch (gluten-free)	Thailand
Mung bean noodle (also known as green bean vermicelli, mung bean vermicelli, glass noodle, cellophane noodle)	Green mung beans (gluten-free)	Southern China/ Korea
Sweet potato noodle (also known as nongshim miga glass noodle)	Sweet potato noodle with tapioca starch (gluten-free)	Southern China/ Korea
Soba noodle (also known as buckwheat noodle)	Buckwheat noodle (gluten-free, but sometimes made with added wheat)	Japan/ Korean
Wonton noodle pastry wrappers (also known as dumpling wrappers)	Wheat (and sometimes egg) noodle	China

THE NOODLE COOKBOOK

DESCRIPTION	GREAT FOR	TASTE + TEXTURE
Rice-based noodle, ranging from super thin to medium—thick. Widely available in supermarkets. You'll get better quality from an east Asian supermarket.	Soup/ Stir-fry/ Stews/ Fried crispy noodle	Bite depends on thickness, liquid and cooking time: thin vermicelli is soft and silky; and thicker varieties used in stir-fries have more bite.
Rice-based noodle, ranging from super-thin to medium—thick. Hard to find: look for them in high-quality or gourmet east Asian supermarkets.	Soup only	Soft and silky texture.
Usually dried, but occasionally fresh. Rectangular shaped small sheet of thin rice noodle – used for wraps or as cake noodle. Look for them in larger east Asian supermarkets, or buy online.	Wraps only	These little sheets absorb flavour, and offer soft texture with little bite.
Flat, thick fresh rice noodle, slightly thinner than ho fun. Can also be frozen, but tastes best when eaten as fresh as possible. Available in east Asian supermarket fridges or freezers.	Stir-fry/ Soup	Smooth and slightly toothsome noodle. Similar to ho fun, can be used as a substitute.
Dried noodle (sometimes available as sheets), looks like glass threads. Widely available in Chinese and other supermarkets.	Soups/ Stir-fry/ Salad/ Stew/ Deep-fry/ Stuffing	Mild-flavoured, rather toothsome thin noodle, but this depends on the way it is cooked.
Round medium-thick, glassy looking and slightly grey in colour. Widely available in Chinese and other supermarkets.	Soup/ Stir-fry/ Salad/ Stew	Slippery noodle with a good toothy bite. Great in soups.
Usually dried thin straight noodles, brownish in colour. Widely available in health food shops and supermarkets.	Soup/ Salad	Super healthy dried noodle, common in Japanese and Korean dishes, often chosen for its thicker toothsome qualities.
Usually round or square shaped. Can be yellow with added egg, or paler egg free types. Widely available in Chinese and other Asian supermarkets.	Dumplings/ Noodle soups/ Crackers	Perfect to make easy dumplings. Also great in soups, or lightly fried to make crispy wonton crackers.

Shopping Staples

The best cookbooks are sauce-stained, well-thumbed and may even rock a few scorch marks. The point is, the best cookbooks are used. One of the things that puts people off trying new recipes is not having the basics in the cupboard: you get all excited about Thai Green Curry, but then find that you're missing some basic ingredients? It's rubbish. So we've put together a few essentials to take with you on your noodle journey. Try hitting a good-quality east Asian supermarket to grab a few long-life essentials. Once you've stocked up on this lot, all you need is a few veggies and some protein, and you're good to go. When selecting meat, we recommend choosing free-range, grass fed and/or organic where possible.

EVERYDAY ESSENTIALS

Healthy cooking oil – There are many different types of oils, but you're looking for one that can take a high cooking temperature, because your wok is going to be hotter than hot and cooking up a storm. Avocado oil is the healthiest because it has those mega omega oils. Rapeseed, peanut and toasted sesame oil are all good and bring a bit of flavour. Any vegetable or olive oil is a good option too, but don't use virgin oils – they don't like the heat. And definitely steer clear of any oils that use non-specific blends or palm oil.

Light soy sauce and tamari – There are some good soy sauces and some not-so-good (we recommend going with good). Look for soy sauce that only has three or four ingredients – and nothing weird, like sodium benzoate. It may be labelled light soy or just soy sauce. Kikkoman soy sauce is a pretty decent bet, as is Healthy Boy (a Thai brand). Soy sauce isn't gluten-free, but most tamari sauces are because they're made differently, so they're a good alternative.

Dark soy sauce – A deeper, saltier flavour than its lighter cousin. Once opened, keep in the fridge and it'll last for months.

Miso paste – Miso is miraculous stuff. Even though all types of miso are all made from fermented soy beans, they can be quite different. White miso is pretty mellow, brown is earthy, and red is the bold-tasting bad boy. Miso is a live cultured product, so to get all that live goodness into your belly, add it to stocks and sauces after boiling.

Fish sauce – You'll find this uniquely flavoured sauce in dishes all over Asia. Made from fermenting fish or krill, so if you have a shellfish allergy, we'd strongly recommend avoiding shop-bought fish sauce. But never fear, Mr Lee has your back. We've included a lovely plant-based alternative on page 25. There are lots of different types of fish sauce, and some countries have their own special blends, such as the PDO-stamped

Vietnamese nước mắm. Good-quality supermarket fish sauces include Red Boat (US), Thai Kitchen (US and Europe) and Squid Brand (Europe).

Sake – Sake serves the same purpose in Asian cooking as white wine does in Western cooking: it adds a bit of sweet flavour and depth to sauces and marinades. If you're buying sake just to drink, rather than to cook with, it's worth looking at some of the premium brands online.

Toasted sesame oil – Nutty and earthy, this lovely oil can transform a dish. It's quite happy at high temperatures and will last for months.

Coconut milk – It's worth reading the small print when it comes to coconut milk. Some tins are stuffed with emulsifiers and fillers and very little actual coconut. That's coconutty if you ask us! Look for tins with at least 85 per cent coconut. You can also use creamed coconut, which comes in a solid block that melts in hot water. Asian supermarkets tend to have powdered coconut milk, too, which is really good.

SOMETIMES STAPLES

Crushed yellow bean sauce – A hit of tinned umami loveliness. This often comes in big tins, so once you've used what you need, you can freeze the rest in an ice-cube tray. But don't accidentally drop them into your G&T – that would be . . . interesting.

Chilli bean paste (toban djan) – This goes by many names: Sichuan broad bean paste, toban djan, chilli paste. This punchy little paste brings the heat to loads of marinades, as well as Chinese dishes like the Dan Dan Noodles on page 70.

Mushroom soy sauce – Somewhere between light and dark soy sauces, this enriched soy sauce has enhanced flavours of straw mushrooms and sometimes shiitake. Makes a great fish-free substitute for oyster sauce.

Mirin – A bit like sake, but less boozy, and with more sweetness. Japanese mirin brings light sweetness and balance to sauces and marinades. It's a nice counterbalance to salty soy and tamari sauces.

Doenjang (Korean fermented soy bean paste) – This versatile fermented soy bean paste has a richly distinct flavour and can be used in a variety of Korean dishes, as well as being a plant-based substitute for fish sauce or miso. Look out for the brown square tub, usually next to the Korean red pepper paste (gochujang) on the shelf.

Sichuan peppercorns – Mouth-tingling-marvels. Look for the more vibrant red ones for the best flavour.

Dried seaweed – Seaweed brings some serious nutrients and flavours to any dish. There are loads of different types, like nori (the sheets used in sushi), wakame and kombu (which is dried kelp, commonly used in making Japanese stocks like dashi). You can find them all pretty easily these days, and there are even some European and American seaweeds to try out, like dulse and laver.

Japanese sesame sauce – This thick, dark sesame paste brings deep, earthy nuttiness to loads of dishes. You can use dark tahini paste instead, but the seeds aren't roasted, so the flavour isn't as full on.

Togarashi spice (Japanese Seven-Spice or Shichimi) – This is a versatile spice mix and seasoning for soups (togarashi means peppers). The shichi-mi type usually contains red chilli, sansho pepper, dried orange or yuzu peel, black and white sesame seeds, ground ginger, poppy or hemp seeds and nori seaweed. You can make a similar flavoured blend as a substitute using ½ teaspoon paprika, ½ teaspoon dried chilli flakes and ¼ teaspoon of toasted sesame seeds.

Shrimp paste – This is an incredible flavour enhancer, so use it sparingly. Shrimp paste punches up anything with umami goodness in all the right places. Keep it in an airtight tub, unless you want your entire fridge to smell like the bottom of the sea (and not in a good way).

Lemongrass stalks – You'll find these citrussy sticks in any supermarket, but you'll find the best ones in speciality supermarkets. You can freeze lemongrass sticks whole, so it's worth buying a bunch for the freezer.

Kaffir lime leaves – For the real deal, go with frozen leaves over dried. They give you the best hit of limey South East Asian goodness. You'll always find a big packet in a Chinese supermarket freezer. If you're stuck with dried, squeeze some lime juice into the dish to give it a flavour boost.

Dried mushrooms – Chinese and shiitake mushrooms will keep for months in the cupboard, and they give any stock or soup some deep umami intensity. Generic Chinese mushrooms are fairly flavourful, whereas shiitake is a very special Japanese mushroom with intense levels of flavour and nutrition.

Tamarind pulp/paste – You'll see these appearing in lots of different forms in the supermarket. It can get a bit confusing, so let's get into it. Tamarind pulp is a thick and runny liquid that is light to mid-brown in colour and should only contain 100 per cent tamarind. This can be easily confused with bottled tamarind sauce, which usually contains lots of sugar. Sometimes this is labelled as paste, but is often visibly more sauce like. You can also get tamarind concentrate or paste, which

is thick, almost set and black. You'll usually find it in little tubs. Great for adding flavour to curries and sauces, but avoid using the dark concentrate type instead of the pulp/sauce type in traditional South East Asian classics like Pad Thai or Tom Yum.

Korean red pepper paste (gochujang) – This sweet and spicy fermented red pepper paste is a signature flavour of many popular Korean dishes. It usually comes in a plastic red tub. If it's from Korea, it will be labelled gochujang, but if it's Chinese, it will usually just be labelled 'red pepper paste'.

Korean red chilli flakes (gochugaru) – these red chilli flakes are a little different to the standard variety, with a unique mild, smoky flavour and gentle, tingly heat. You can find them online and in specialist Asian supermarkets.

RECIPE KEY

Difficulty scale	1 – DODDLE 2 – A LITTLE EFFORT 3 – SHOWING OFF
One-Wok Wonder	Can be made using only one pan.
Gluten-Free/ Vegetarian/ Vegan (Option)	Recipe either is or can be adapted to be meat-free, plant-based or gluten-free. If you're using any pre-prepared ingredients, always check the ingredients on the packaging.
<15 min	Recipe goes from wok to plate in less than 15 minutes. Speedy suppers!

Healthy Alternatives

We're all about food that works for you and your diet. So we've come up with lots of healthy alternatives that still pack in the flavour. We've got some crowd-pleasing, homemade, healthy store-cupboard recipes on pages 24–29, but below are some good off-the-shelf alternatives that have the Mr Lee's seal of approval. Always check the ingredients label if you have any dietary requirements.

Tamari – Similar to light soy sauce, except lower in salt and has higher concentration of soy beans (so higher in protein). Usually non-wheat filtered. Always check the label.

Coconut aminos – A gluten- and soy-free substitute for soy sauce, containing 17 amino acids, as well as potassium and vitamins C and B.

Agave syrup – A low-GI, plant-based alternative to sugar, made from the South American agave plant.

Honey – Another low-GI alternative to sugar. Good-quality honey also packs in the antioxidants.

Healthy tomato ketchup (no added sugar) – A good, healthy choice, and much better than low-sugar ketchups that contain artificial sweeteners.

Healthy peanut butter – Look out for no-added sugar brands.

Mock meat alternatives – A widely available option if you're looking to eat a more plant-based diet. Look out for alternatives to meat and seafood such as tofu, green jackfruit, seitan (a mock meat made from wheat gluten), Quorn (a myco-protein), heart of palm, soy steaks and many more.

Hero Ingredients

Throughout this book you'll find some recipes that include one (or more) very special ingredient. There are super-healthy amazing hero foods that go above and beyond. Here's why.

Seaweed
Each type of seaweed has its own set of nutrients. Most are high in natural iron, manganese, copper and B vitamins (one study found nori is a super source of the elusive B12). It's also a concentrated source of iodine and an amino acid called tyrosine, which supports healthy thyroid function.

Sesame seeds/sauce/oil
A fantastic source of fibre and plant protein, and high in minerals and vitamins, including iron, copper, calcium (unhulled), selenium (good for eyes and thyroid), manganese, magnesium, vitamin B6 and phytoestrogens. As if that wasn't enough, sesame also helps lower cholesterol, triglycerides and blood pressure. How good is that?

Buckwheat
Naturally gluten-free, this lovely little grain is high in dietary fibre, easily digestible protein, antioxidants, magnesium, iron and B vitamins.

Garlic
Garlic is the Jason Statham of the vegetable world because it fights everything from heart disease and cholesterol to arthritis and cancer – probably with a round-house kick and a quippy one-liner.

Chilli
Chilli heat is measured by the Scoville Scale that measures the capsaicin levels, a susbstance that gives chilli peppers their pungency and heat. Chillies help fight inflammation and provide natural pain relief. Other benefits include cardiovascular improvements, clearing congestion and boosting immunity.

THE NOODLE COOKBOOK

9560000251623

Sardines
These little fishies are packed with omega-3 fatty acids, which help prevent heart disease. They're also a brilliant source of vitamin B12 and calcium.

Bananas
Ah, the humble banana. A great natural sweetener and high in potassium, magnesium and vitamins C and B6. Probably shouldn't be so humble.

Spinach (and other leafy greens)
These leafy legends contains more nutrients than any other vegetable! A great source of vitamins A, B2, B6, C and E, as well as manganese, folate, magnesium, iron, copper and potassium.

Miso
Marvellous miso! Rich in essential minerals and a great source of various B vitamins, as well as vitamins E and K, and folic acid. It's fermented, so is rich in beneficial bacteria for a healthy gut, which is known to benefit our overall mental and physical wellbeing.

Green jackfruit
Often used as a healthy meat alternative in curries and noodle soups. This low-carb South East Asian tree fruit is a good source of antioxidants, vitamin C, potassium and dietary fibre.

Tofu
Often used as a healthy meat alternative in West and in Asian food, more commonly combined with seafood or pork, in stir-fry, curry and noodle soup. High in protein and low in fat, it contains all nine essential amino acids and is a good source of iron, calcium and other trace minerals.

Turmeric
Terrific turmeric contains the active compound curcumin, which has been scientifically proven to help prevent heart disease, Alzheimer's and cancer. It's also a potent anti-inflammatory and antioxidant, and may help relieve symptoms of depression and arthritis.

Walnuts
Rich in antioxidants and a super source of omega-3 fats – the walnut is the GOAT (greatest of all time) of nuts. It also promotes healthy gut health and may help decrease inflammation and the risk of some cancers, due to its high levels of polyphenols.

Peppercorns
The king of spices! Peppercorns are super-high in antioxidants and the active compound piperine, shown to benefit brain function, blood sugar metabolism and cholesterol levels. It has even been shown to have cancer-fighting properties.

Lemongrass
Sometimes used medicinally to calm tummies and ease muscle pain and cold symptoms. Lemongrass also contains lots of minerals.

Kimchi
Very tasty and packed with good bacteria and healthy probiotics to support gut health and overall wellness.

Salmon
A low-fat, omega-3-rich protein, packed with those elusive B vitamins.

Ginger
Ginger is well-respected in medicine. Antibacterial, anti-emetic (eases nausea), anti-inflammatory and it lowers both cholesterols and blood sugars.

Coconut water
A lovely light and healthy natural sweetener for soups and broths, coconut water has essential minerals and also supports heart and kidney health. It also helps control blood sugars.

Coconut milk/cream
A high calorie food. Contrary to popular belief, coconut milk helps increase HDL levels (good cholesterol and decrease LDL levels (bad cholesterol). Known to improve blood pressure and is a good source of potassium.

Cinnamon
Well known for its anti-inflammatory properties and goodness for heart and insulin levels, cinnamon is also packed with antioxidants. Plus, it's Christmassy.

Shiitake mushrooms
Holy Shiitake! These cracking little shrooms may help fight cancer, boost immunity and support heart health.

Pineapple
Punchy pineapple packs high amounts of vitamin C and manganese, as well as dietary fibre and the enzyme bromelain, which helps the body heal itself. Sweet!

Squid
A brilliant source of B vitamins, important for neural health, and also vitamin E and selenium, which work together to support eye health, body growth and fertility. Squid-tastic!

Mussels
Mussels have less than a third of the cholesterol found in prawns, and boast a much higher nutrient density (especially potassium, iron and vitamins B12 and C). Take that, prawns! (Although we do love a prawn.)

Oysters
An incredibly nutrient-rich form of protein, especially for their B12, omega-3 and mineral content. When farmed sustainably, oysters are also good for the environment.

Mackerel
Mackerel packs super-high levels of essential fatty acids, with double the omega-3 power of salmon. It also contains fewer heavy metals.

Spirulina
A super nutrient-rich seaweed, containing all the essential amino acids.

Goji berry
A fantastic source of vitamins and minerals, this brilliant berry is also famous for its anti-ageing benefits and immune function support.

Anchovies
Super-high in omega-3s, which decrease inflammation and maintain cell health, anchovies are also rich in B-complex vitamins. They're lovely on pizza, too (although that's a whole different book).

Broccoli
A great source of fibre and protein, broccoli also contains iron, potassium, calcium, selenium and magnesium as well as vitamins A, C, E and K, and a good array of B vitamins, including folic acid. Brilliant broccoli!

Edamame
Edamame could be the most perfect unprocessed plant-based protein; rich in antioxidants and vitamin K. They may also reduce the risk of heart disease and improve cholesterol and triglycerides.

Plant-based milk
A brilliant alternative to dairy for everyone. Most plant-based milks are rich in vitamins and minerals, low in fat and contain no cholesterol!

Heart of palm
A lovely low-carb, healthy alternative to seafood and in salads. Very popular in North and South America, and widely available in tins.

Crayfish tails
Super-tasty and high in B vitamins and minerals like calcium, magnesium, iron, zinc and phosphorus. Also high in protein, and a more sustainable option than farmed prawns.

Enoki mushrooms
The world's fourth most popular mushroom, apparently. Still brilliant, though. It contains an array of nutrients, including vitamins B3, B5, B1 and B2 as well as phosphorus, iron, selenium, thiamin, calcium and copper.

Red cabbage
Contains 10 times more vitamins and cancer-fighting flavonoids than green cabbage, together with a huge dose of vitamin C and powerful antioxidant rich immune-system booster.

Bell peppers
Low calorie and nutrient-rich, these lovelies contain a healthy dose of fibre, folate and iron. Also a great source of vitamins A, C and potassium.

Healthy Store Cupboard Recipes

MR LEE'S HEALTHY MUSSEL SAUCE

GLUTEN-FREE OPTION

Fish sauce is often packed with rubbish chemicals. Keep this healthy little beauty in a sterilised bottle in the fridge for up to 2 weeks.

Makes approx. 40ml (1½fl oz)

—

800g (1lb 12oz) fresh mussels, shells on
½ teaspoon dark soy sauce, or use (or 1 teaspoon taamari for a gluten-free alternative)
½ teaspoon honey or agave syrup

Prepare the mussels by getting rid of any that stay open after a light tapping. Then remove the beards by pinching and firmly pulling them away from the shell.

Pop the mussels into a large saucepan. Cover with the lid and cook for 2 minutes over a very high heat. Stir, then reduce the heat to medium and cook for another 2 minutes. Drain the mussels using a sieve, and keep the liquid.

Pour the remaining liquid back into the saucepan and cook for 10–15 minutes until it has reduced to about 2 tablespoons, then add the dark soy sauce and honey. Turn off the heat, and the sauce is good to go.

The mussels can be eaten on their own, or why not take them for a spin with Andy's Quick Sweet Chilli Dip (page 25) or Mr Lee's Red Chilli Oil (page 29)?

MR LEE'S SOUTH EAST ASIAN HOT SAUCE

GLUTEN-FREE OPTION / VEGAN OPTION

If you like your chilli heat, this bad boy's got your name on it. It keeps for up to 8 weeks in a sterilised jar in the fridge.

Makes approx. 450ml (16fl oz)

—

40g (1½oz) dried large red chillies, roughly chopped
6 garlic cloves, peeled
300ml (½ pint) cold water
3½ tablespoons ready-made fish sauce, light soy sauce, Mr Lee's Vegan 'Fish' Sauce (page 25) or tamari (for a gluten-free alternative)
50g (1¾oz) coconut sugar, or 50ml (2fl oz) agave syrup
150ml (¼ pint) rice vinegar

Place the chillies, garlic and water in a small saucepan over a medium heat. Bring to the boil and simmer gently for 5–10 minutes.

Take the saucepan off the heat and add the fish sauce (or soy sauce, Vegan 'Fish' Sauce or tamari), along with the coconut sugar or agave syrup and rice vinegar. Blend the mixture using a stick blender, or transfer to a food processor to blend.

Return to the heat and simmer for another 3–4 minutes until starting to thicken. Then leave to cool.

ANDY'S QUICK SWEET CHILLI DIP

GLUTEN-FREE / VEGAN OPTION

Supermarket sweet chilli dips are usually loaded up with refined sugar. So Andy made his own and shared it with you! Good bloke, Andy.

Makes approx. 60ml (2½fl oz)
—

½ small carrot, finely chopped
2 red chillies, finely chopped
½ teaspoon sea salt
½ tablespoon rice vinegar or lemon juice
2 tablespoons honey (or agave syrup,
    for a vegan alternative)

In a small bowl, mix together the carrot, chillies, salt and vinegar or lemon juice. Cover and leave it for 2 minutes, then add the honey (or agave syrup), stir and you're all set. The sauce will keep for up to 3 weeks in a sterilised jar.

MR LEE'S HOISIN SAUCE

Who doesn't love hoisin? We've kept all the loveliness and upped the health.

GLUTEN-FREE OPTION / VEGAN OPTION

Makes approx. 135ml (4½fl oz)
—

4 tablespoons light soy sauce (or tamari,
    for a gluten-free alternative)
2 tablespoons smooth peanut butter
2 tablespoons honey (or agave syrup,
    for a vegan alternative)
2 teaspoons rice vinegar
½ teaspoon garlic paste, or 1 garlic clove,
    crushed and finely chopped
1 teaspoon chilli sauce, either ready-made
    hot chilli sauce or paste, or use Mr Lee's
    South East Asian Hot Sauce (page 24)
large pinch of ground black pepper

Just place all the ingredients in a medium-sized bowl and whisk together until well combined. And that's it! This will keep for 1 month in a sterilised bottle in the fridge.

MR LEE'S HEALTHY TERIYAKI SAUCE

VEGAN OPTION / GLUTEN FREE OPTION

Another one that's laced with sugar if you get it off the shelf. This is much healthier and a doddle to make.

Makes about 75ml (2½fl oz)
—

1 tablespoon light soy sauce, (or substitute
    1 tablespoon gluten free tamari)
½ tablespoon dark soy sauce, (or substitute
    2 teaspoons gluten free tamari)
1 tablespoon sake
1 tablespoon mirin
1 tablespoon honey (or agave syrup,
    for a vegan alternative)
4 tablespoons water
½ teaspoon garlic paste, or 1 garlic clove,
    crushed and finely chopped
½ teaspoon ginger paste or use ground ginger

Simply place all the ingredients in a medium-sized pan and whisk together until well combined. Place in small pan on high heat and bring to simmer, reducing the liquid for 5 minutes. Remove from heat and cool. This will keep for up to a month in a sterilised bottle in the fridge.

MR LEE'S VEGAN 'FISH' SAUCE

GLUTEN-FREE OPTION / VEGAN

Want the fish sauce seasoning without the fish? This brilliant little vegan cheat will sort you out.

Makes 75ml (2½fl oz)
—

½ teaspoon agave syrup
30ml (1fl oz) water
30ml (1fl oz) pineapple juice
30ml (1fl oz) light soy sauce (or
    tamari for a gluten-free alternative)
½–1 teaspoon sea salt, to taste

Simply place all the ingredients in a medium-sized bowl and mix together until well combined. This will keep for a week in the fridge.

MR LEE'S HEALTHY PEANUT SATAY SAUCE

GLUTEN-FREE OPTION / VEGAN OPTION

Super-moreish: you can use it in recipes, as a dipping sauce, as a marinade, or just pour it directly into your mouth!

Makes about 450ml (16fl oz)

400ml (14fl oz) good-quality coconut milk
4–5 tablespoons crunchy peanut butter
    (use one with no added sugar)
1 tablespoon light soy sauce (or use tamari,
    for a gluten-free alternative)
½ tablespoon dried chilli flakes
2 teaspoons honey (or agave syrup for
    a vegan alternative)
1 teaspoon ready-made fish sauce, or Mr Lee's
'Vegan' Fish Sauce (page 25), for a vegan
    and (optional) gluten-free alternative
1 tablespoon almond flour or fine
    ground almonds
½ teaspoon dark soy sauce (optional, to enrich
    the sauce)
sea salt, to taste

Put all the ingredients into a medium-sized bowl and whisk together until well combined.

Transfer the mixture to a small saucepan and place over a low–medium heat. Bring to a gentle simmer for 3–4 minutes, then take off the heat.

Serve warm or let it cool. The sauce will keep for up to 1 week in the fridge.

MR LEE'S SUPER SIMPLE KIMCHI

GLUTEN-FREE / VEGAN OPTION

This classic Korean side is super-healthy and, like any fermented product, packed with good bacteria for maintaining gut health. Kimchi usually takes 3–4 days to ferment after prepping, but will taste at it's best from 10–14 days. It will then last another 2–3 months in the fridge. It's totally worth the wait.

Makes approx. 1 litre (1 ¾ pint)

850g–1kg (1lb 14oz–2lb 4oz) Chinese
    cabbage leaves, roughly chopped into
    2.5–5cm (1–2in) pieces
2 tablespoons sea salt
500ml (18fl oz) cold water
1 apple
180g (6½oz) daikon (also known as mooli or Asian
    radish), sliced into thin 2.5–5cm (1–2in) strips
180g (6½oz) carrot, cut into julienne strips
    or grated
80g (2¾oz) spring onions (scallions),
    finely chopped
100g (3½oz) leek, finely sliced
2.5–5cm (1–2in) piece of fresh root ginger,
    finely chopped
6 garlic cloves, crushed and chopped
1 large onion, finely sliced
2 tablespoons light soy sauce (or use tamari
    for a gluten-free alternative)
2–5 tablespoons Korean red chilli
    flakes (gochugaru)
1 tablespoon honey (or use agave syrup
    for a vegan alternative)

Put the Chinese leaves in a large bowl with the salt and water and mix together. Leave for at least 30 minutes. Then remove the leaves and wash them well under cold running water. Dry them by placing on to a large tea towel, then place them in a large (dry) mixing bowl.

Soak the apple in hot water for 1 minute, then dry. Remove the core and thinly slice, leaving the skin on. Place the apple in another bowl, and add the remaining ingredients. Mix together well, using your hands (wear food-safe gloves).

Pour this mixture into the larger bowl with the Chinese leaves and mix well. Pack all the ingredients into a large sterilised glass jar, leaving 2.5cm (1in) space at the top. Open the jar every 3–4 days, which will release any gas pressure. Store for 3–4 days at a warm room temperature. The longer you wait, the better the flavour will become. After opening, it'll keep in the fridge for up to 3 months.

 Kimchi Mandu with Pork & Mung Bean Noodles (page 178)

MR LEE'S RED CURRY PASTE

GLUTEN-FREE OPTION

We've made this traditional recipe a bit simpler to throw together. Fiery red Thai chillies pack a real punch, so use those if you like it hotter! This recipe will make approximately 100ml (3½fl oz), so just double or quadruple the quantities if you want to make more.

Makes approx. 100ml (3½fl oz)
—

½ tablespoon vegetable oil
1 onion, finely diced
1–2 large red chillies, or 2 tablespoons dried
    red chilli flakes, to taste
1 lemongrass stalk, finely chopped
2 teaspoons garlic paste, or 4 garlic cloves, peeled
1 teaspoon galangal powder, or use ginger
    paste or ground ginger
2 tablespoons no-added-sugar tomato ketchup
1 teaspoon ground cumin
1 teaspoon ground coriander
¼ teaspoon ground white pepper
2 tablespoons Mr Lee's Healthy Mussel Sauce
    (page 24), or ready-made fish sauce
1 tablespoon shrimp paste
1 teaspoon honey or agave syrup

Heat the oil in a wok over a medium–high heat. Add the onion and cook for 6–8 minutes until softened. Add the chillies or chilli flakes, lemongrass and garlic, and cook for another 3–4 minutes. Then add the remaining ingredients and mix together to make a rough paste.

If you have a stick blender or food processor, simply transfer the cooked mixture and blend using that.

You can freeze this fresh paste, or store it for up to a month in a sterilised jar in the fridge.

MR LEE'S RED CHILLI OIL

GLUTEN-FREE / VEGAN

Drizzle this over just about everything to bring the heat.

Makes approx. 50 ml
—

2 tablespoons dried chilli flakes
½ tablespoon paprika
½ teaspoon Chinese five-spice powder
¼ teaspoon sea salt
2 tablespoons vegetable oil

Place the chilli flakes, paprika, five-spice powder and salt in a heatproof bowl and mix well.

Heat the vegetable oil in a saucepan over a medium heat until hot, but don't let it boil. Remove from the heat and pour the oil into the bowl with the dried ingredients. Stir, then leave to cool for 5 minutes, and it's ready to use. It will keep for a month in a sterilised jar.

*Turkey-Stuffed Wonton Noodle Pastry
with Red Chilli Oil (page 96)*

TOASTING SESAME SEEDS

Freshly toasted sesame seeds make a gorgeous finishing touch to many noodle dishes. Use them when you want to add a touch of specialness.

Makes 100g (3½oz)
—

100g (3½oz) white sesame seeds

Half-fill a small saucepan with boiling water and bring to the boil over a medium heat. Add the sesame seeds and boil for 30 seconds, then strain using a fine sieve and rinse with cold water.

Pour the sesame seeds into a dry frying pan over a medium heat. Stir constantly until the seeds are golden brown and start popping. Store in an airtight container once cooled. They will keep for up to 6 months.

MAKING TOFU TASTY

In the West, tofu can be looked down on by committed carnivores. Not so in Asian cooking. This protein powerhouse is often used to complement seafood and pork – or to replace them altogether! The key is prep: get that right, and you have yourself some tasty tofu.

Silken tofu is the super-soft variety you often find floating around your miso soup. It's not for everyone. Look out for firm tofu, which usually comes in a block. This has much more texture and soaks up all the flavours of the rest of the dish. If you want to make it a little firmer still, freeze it first and then fully defrost, squeezing out all the water. This will actually change the structure of the protein, and the texture will become meatier.

By itself, tofu doesn't taste of much, so be generous with flavouring and seasoning. You can bake or fry pieces of tofu to make more toothsome nuggets to add to dishes or to replace chicken or seafood. Baked tofu is crispy-edged and gives you a bit more texture. Tofu puffs, the deep-fried kind that you can find in the fridge at the Chinese supermarkets or floating around in a big bowl of laksa, are chewy, saucy-filled little wonders.

Pancake Tacos with Kimchi Salsa (page 166)

These are our absolute favourites. Some remind us of our parents, some were random discoveries on a bustling, steamy street in a far-off land, some have been passed on to us by friends, handwritten and sauce-stained. But they all have one thing in common: these are the dishes we turn to when we want to taste something a bit special.

This is the place to come if you want a first-date icebreaker or a 'meeting the mother-in-law' showstopper. We've got you covered if you want to ditch the soggy sarnies with some clever lunchtime hacks, or whip up a feast for the senses for a bunch of mates. It's all here.

In standard Mr Lee's style, we've given these dishes our own twist: taking a bit of East, a bit of West, mixing it up and making something brand new, yet comfortingly familiar. They're all super-healthy, low-fat, low-salt and balanced with gorgeous veggies and proteins. And you can knock them all up in 30 minutes or less with our cheeky shortcuts and clever twists. Eating well has never been so easy.

1

Mr Lee's Asian Favourites

- Serves 2
- A Little Effort / Vegan Option
- Wok to wonderful in 30 minutes
- Hero ingredient: turmeric (page 21)

Spicy Malaysian Noodle Curry (Mee Rebus)

Silky Street Food Sensation

Chinese-Malay cooking is famous for how it beautifully combines sweetness with the deeply savoury. The silky curry sauce is a gorgeous combo of sweet potato, tomato and fermented soy bean. Traditionally, you'd serve this with a boiled egg, but you can make it vegan with egg-free yellow noodles. We're using chicken or tofu, but prawns are good too.

1 packet of dried Hokkien egg noodles (or use dried thick round rice vermicelli noodles, for a vegan alternative)

1 tablespoon vegetable oil

1 red onion, finely diced

1 tablespoon dried red chilli flakes

2 tablespoons ginger paste, or 2–3cm (¾–1¼in) piece of fresh root ginger, finely chopped

1½ teaspoons ground turmeric

3 teaspoons garlic paste, or 4 garlic cloves, finely chopped

2 tablespoons brown soy bean paste, or brown or red miso

3 sweet potatoes, peeled and chopped

3 ripe tomatoes, cored and chopped

1 litre (1¾ pints) vegetable stock

½ tablespoon honey (or use agave syrup for a vegan alternative)

1 teaspoon sea salt, or to taste

220g (7¾oz) cooked chicken breast, chopped into bite-sized pieces (or use ½ block of firm tofu, diced, for a vegan alternative)

100g (3½oz) bean sprouts (optional)

8 cherry tomatoes, halved

lime wedges, to serve

Mr Lee's Red Chilli Oil (page 29), optional, to serve

Soak the noodles in a bowl or pan of boiling water for 10–15 minutes, or according to the packet instructions. Drain and set aside until needed.

Heat the oil in a large wok over a medium–high heat. Add the onion and fry for a few minutes to soften it up. Add the chilli flakes, ginger, turmeric, garlic, and soy bean paste to the pan and mix well. Cook for another 2–3 minutes, stirring. The smell should be making you hungry at this stage!

Add the sweet potatoes, vegetable stock and chopped tomatoes (not the cherry ones). Bring to a simmer and cook for 15 minutes until the vegetables are nice and soft, then remove from the heat.

Blitz the mixture with a stick blender, if you have one, until smooth and silky. Alternatively, use a potato masher and squash the mixture to make a pulpy soup base. Really go for it, it's a good workout! Add the salt and honey or agave syrup to taste. Add the chicken or tofu, along with the bean sprouts and cherry tomatoes. Return the pan to the heat and bring back to a simmer, then remove from the heat again.

Divide the noodles between 2 bowls and ladle over the sauce. Top with a wedge of lime and a drizzle of red chilli oil if you like.

● Serves 2 as starter
or light meal

● A Little Effort / Vegan

● Wok to wonderful in
22 minutes

● Hero ingredient:
cinnamon (page 22)

Vietnamese Stuffed Rice Noodle Wraps

Family-feasting-finger-licking-winner

If you're ever invited to a family feast in Vietnam, we don't care what you had planned, GO. You'll be very well fed. These are usually served alongside suckling pig. You can find the rectangle-shaped thin rice noodle cake in Asian supermarkets, but you can use small corn tortillas instead. Lay out the bits and pieces and the diners assemble the dish as they want. They do all the work; you take all the credit.

1 large field or Portobello mushroom, peeled and thickly sliced

¼ teaspoon Chinese five-spice powder

½ tablespoon vegetable oil

1 celery stalk, stringy parts removed (see Tip), cut into 5cm (2in) sticks

pinch or two of sea salt

½ medium carrot, peeled and cut into 5cm (2in) sticks

2 pinches of ground cinnamon

6–8 fine rice vermicelli sheets

¼ teaspoon dried chilli flakes

4 tablespoons Mr Lee's Hoisin Sauce (page 25), or ready-made hoisin sauce (check the ingredients if you're vegan)

Lay the sliced mushrooms on a chopping board or a large plate and sprinkle with the five-spice powder. Next, heat the vegetable oil in a large frying pan (skillet) over a high heat. Lay the mushroom slices in the pan and fry for 1 minute on each side, until the edges become nicely golden brown. Remove from the pan and set aside in a small bowl.

Keeping the pan over a high heat, add the celery pieces, along with a pinch of salt. Fry for 1 minute, stirring well, then set aside in a small bowl. Then return the pan to the heat once again and add the carrot sticks, together with a pinch of sea salt and the ground cinnamon. Mix well and fry for 1 minute. Then set aside in a small bowl.

Lay out the noodle sheets in a deep baking tray or wide dish, making sure the sheets aren't touching. Pour over boiling water to cover and leave to soak for 2 minutes.

Arrange the vegetables in their small bowls, and sprinkle the chilli flakes on top of the celery. Pop the hoisin sauce in another small bowl.

Finally, lift the noodle sheets out of the tray and drain the excess water, then lay the sheets on a serving plate or board alongside all the filling ingredients.

To eat, lay a noodle wrapper on one hand and top with a bit of everything, followed by a generous drizzle of hoisin sauce. Roll the sheet to make a stuffed roll and eat immediately. Better be quick – these puppies disappear fast.

● **Tip:** To remove the stringy parts of the celery stalk, just pinch the end of the stalk and peel lengthways, pulling away the stringy outer part. Repeat this pinch-and-pull technique several times at both ends of the stalk to remove all the string.

THE NOODLE COOKBOOK

- Serves 2 as starter or light meal
- Doddle / <15 Min / Vegan
- Wok to wonderful in 10 minutes
- Hero ingredients: buckwheat and plant-based milk (page 20/23)

MR LEE'S ASIAN FAVOURITES

Creamy Soba Noodles with Baby Corn

Corny Comfort Food

Tasty and healthy soba or buckwheat noodles are very popular in Japan. When all these flavours come together, you've got something really comforting that makes you feel better about everything. Use an unsweetened milk and bear in mind the fat content: the higher the fat content, the creamier the flavour. So, for maximum creaminess, go with soy milk.

285g/10oz fresh soba noodles (or use dried wholewheat noodles or spaghetti)

4 pieces of baby corn, fresh or frozen, sliced at an angle into 1–2cm (½–¾in) pieces

1 spring onion (scallion), finely sliced, to serve

FOR THE SAUCE:

1 tablespoon mirin

½ tablespoon tamari

1 teaspoon red miso paste, or any miso of your choice

1 teaspoon toasted sesame oil

¼ teaspoon finely ground white pepper

400ml (14fl oz) unsweetened soy, oat or almond milk

Mix all the sauce ingredients together in a saucepan and place it over a medium–high heat. Bring to the boil, then add the noodles and baby corn, simmering for 2 minutes. Keep stirring so that nothing catches.

Once the noodles and baby corn are cooked through, pour the soup into bowls and serve, sprinkled with the spring onion (scallion) to garnish. How simple is that?

Thai-spiced Wild Salmon Noodle Cakes

Small but Mighty

It's amazing what you can do with some tinned fish and fragrant Thai flavours. We've used vermicelli noodles, so you'll get lots of crispy bits making sweet music with the succulent, spiced omega-rich fish and brilliant dipping sauces. The veggie version substitutes the fish for heart of palm, a low-carb South American vegetable which you'll find in most high street supermarkets.

50g (1¾oz) dried rice vermicelli noodles
2 tablespoons vegetable oil
1 small onion or banana shallot, finely chopped
1 tablespoon Mr Lee's Red Curry Paste (page 29), or use a ready-made vegetarian red curry paste
2 teaspoons cornflour (corn starch), plus extra for dusting
handful of freshly chopped coriander (cilantro)
½ teaspoon fine sea salt
3 tablespoons panko breadcrumbs
170g (6oz) tin wild salmon, or tinned line-caught tuna or crab, if you prefer, drained (or, for a vegetarian option, use 170g/6oz tinned heart of palms, drained and patted dry)

FOR THE PANKO COATING:
1 egg, beaten
90g (3¼oz) panko breadcrumbs

TO SERVE (OPTIONAL):
handful of lettuce leaves
Andy's Quick Sweet Chilli Dip (page 25) and Mr Lee's South East Asian Hot Sauce (page 24)
lime wedges

Place the noodles in a bowl of boiling water and leave to stand for 5 minutes until softened, then drain. Once cool enough to handle, chop the drained noodles with scissors to make shorter pieces, then set aside.

Heat ½ tablespoon of the vegetable oil in a small frying pan (skillet) over a medium–high heat. Add the onion or shallot and fry for 8 minutes until softened but not browned. Add the curry paste and cook for 2 minutes, then take off the heat.

In a large mixing bowl, mix together the cooked onion or shallot, cornflour (corn starch), coriander (cilantro), salt and 3 tablespoons panko breadcrumbs. Add the chopped noodles. Using your hands (you should wear food-safe gloves for this bit), mix it all really well to combine. Really get stuck in, squeezing slightly to help it form a dough, then fold in the flaked fish or heart of palms.

Form the dough into 6–8 little patties and dust with a little cornflour.

For the coating, place the beaten egg in a bowl, and the panko bread crumbs in a shallow dish or plate. One at a time, dip the patties in the beaten egg, then roll them in the breadcrumbs to give them a nice even panko crust. It's all good, messy fun!

Place a large frying pan over a medium–high heat with the remaining 1½ tablespoons oil. Shallow-fry the patties, in batches, for 4 minutes on each side until they are golden brown. Set aside on a plate lined with paper towels to drain.

Serve the cakes on top of a few lettuce leaves, with the dipping sauces and lime wedges on the side.

Lobster Laksa Curry
Luxury Lushness

A brilliant laksa is all about the broth. Spicy, fragrant, coconutty and glowing with turmeric, it should be bowl-lickingly-lovely. You'll find cracking laksas all over South East Asia, from Bali to Malaysia and beyond. It's typically served with yellow or rice noodles and loads of toppings. We've luxed it up with some lobster, but you can substitute with unshelled prawns.

120–150g (4–5½oz) dried thin or medium rice vermicelli noodles
1 cooked lobster (350g–500g/12oz–1lb 2oz), or approx. 400g (14 oz) raw, shell-on prawns
400ml (14fl oz) boiling water
8 frozen queen scallops, or 3 king scallops, halved or quartered
1 tablespoon Mr Lee's Healthy Mussel Sauce (page 24), or ready-made fish sauce
200ml (7fl oz) coconut milk
1 teaspoon dried chilli flakes
200g (7oz) bean sprouts
1 teaspoon honey or agave syrup

FOR THE SPICE PASTE:
2 anchovy fillets, finely chopped (from a jar)
1 onion, chopped
2 teaspoons ginger paste, or 5cm (2in) piece of fresh root ginger, finely chopped
2 garlic cloves, crushed and finely chopped
1 lemongrass stalk, finely chopped, or 2 teaspoons ground dried lemongrass
1 tablespoon freshly chopped coriander (cilantro)
2.5cm (1 in) piece of fresh turmeric, finely chopped, or 1¼ teaspoons ground turmeric
1 teaspoon tamarind paste or pulp
½ teaspoon ground cumin
½ teaspoon paprika

TO SERVE:
5cm (2in) piece of cucumber, cut into batons
1–2 red bird's-eye chillies, finely sliced
small handful of fresh coriander (cilantro), or mint if you prefer
small handful of bean sprouts
lime wedges

Soak the rice noodles for 10 minutes in warm water, then drain and set aside.

Next prepare your seafood. This might get a bit messy – just embrace it! If you're using lobster, firmly grip the head in one hand and the body in the other. Pull the head firmly away, then remove the legs and the rest of the shell from the meat. Rinse the meat and shells in cold water if you need to. The claws can be tricky little blighters, so you might need to use a nutcracker or hammer to break them open. Set aside the cooked tail and claw meat for later, making sure you've caught any bits of shell. If you're using raw prawns, pull off the heads and peel the shells. You can add the heads and large pieces of shell to the spice paste at the next stage. Set aside the raw prawn meat to cook later.

To make the spice paste, place a large wok over a high heat and add the chopped anchovies and onion to the pan. Lower the heat to medium and fry for 2 minutes, until the onion has softened, then add the remaining spice paste ingredients to the pan, mixing well. Cook for another minute.

Next, add the lobster or prawn head(s) and large shell pieces (only use the large ones, as you'll need to fish them out later). The shells will bring another level

of flavour to your broth. Increase the heat to high and mix well. Then add the boiling water and bring to a simmer over a medium heat. Cook for 15 minutes. We're looking to get as much flavour into that broth as we can.

After 15 minutes, remove all the pieces of shell and the lobster or prawn head(s). Then add the scallops, mussel or fish sauce, coconut milk and chilli flakes and bring the broth back to a simmer. Next add the lobster or prawn meat. Now add the cooked noodles, along with the bean sprouts and honey or agave. Mix it all up, remove from the heat and taste the broth. Adjust the seasoning, adding more fish sauce if you like.

To serve, divide the noodles, seafood and broth between two large bowls. Top each bowl with cucumber batons, sliced chillies, coriander (cilantro), bean sprouts and a wedge of lime. Grab your chopsticks and imagine yourself drinking in the sights, sounds and smells of Kuala Lumpur.

Chilli-bean Glazed Sea Bass with Fresh Rice Noodles

Red Hot Chilli Bass Player

Why nuke a ready meal when you can have succulent fish, crispy skin and tongue-warming spices in just 12 minutes? The marinade is super-simple, using Sichuan-style fermented chilli bean paste, known as toban djan. Pro tip: to get that restaurant-quality crispy skin, get your frying pan 'surface-of-the-sun' hot.

100g (3½oz) fresh sea bass fillet, skin on (or you can use frozen – just defrost it thoroughly first)

½–1 teaspoon sea salt

few pinches of ground white pepper

2 teaspoons chilli bean paste (toban djan)

½ tablespoon vegetable oil

1 red onion, finely sliced

200g (7oz) fresh thin rice noodles, or 60g (2¼oz) dried mung bean noodles

½ tablespoon light soy sauce

½ tablespoon mirin

½ spring onion (scallion), green part only

½ fresh red or green chilli, deseeded and cut into thin strips (optional)

Before you begin, stick on your favourite Red Hot Chili Peppers playlist (optional).

Score the skin of the sea bass three times with a sharp knife. Season the skin side of the sea bass with a pinch of salt and pepper, then spread the chilli bean sauce or paste on the flesh side and let it stand for a minute.

Heat the oil in a large frying pan (skillet) over a high heat. When it's smoking hot, carefully place the sea bass fillet, skin-side down, in the hot pan. Cook for 3 minutes. Take the pan off the heat, turn the fish over and let it sit in the hot pan for another 3 minutes to cook the other side, then carefully remove the fish from the pan and let it rest.

Next, place the same pan back over a high heat, add the sliced red onion and fry for 30 seconds. Then add the noodles, mirin and soy sauce, and mix well. Stir-fry for 2 minutes.

Once cooked, tip the noodles on to a large plate and top with the sea bass fillet, crispy skin side facing up. Scatter with spring onion (scallion) slices and fresh chilli strips, then tuck in.

- Serves 2
- A Little Effort / Gluten-Free Option
- Wok to wonderful in 25 minutes
- Hero ingredient: mackerel (page 22)

Penang Hot & Sour Noodle Soup with Mackerel

Smack Your Lips Up!

Originally from Penang, this fiery little number carefully balances the sweet and sour of the tamarind with the beautifully savoury sweet oily fish. It's worth tracking down some good-quality 100 per cent tamarind pulp, which will take it to another level. You can make it gluten-free by using rice noodles instead of egg noodles if you like.

120g (4¼oz) dried thick egg noodles (or use dried thick round rice vermicelli noodles for a gluten-free alternative)
1 tablespoon vegetable oil
1 small red onion, finely diced
½ tablespoon hot chilli paste
½ tablespoon paprika
1 litre (1¾ pints) vegetable stock
1 tablespoon Mr Lee's Healthy Mussel Sauce (page 24) or ready-made fish sauce
2 tablespoons tamarind pulp, or 2 teaspoons tamarind paste
juice of ½ lemon
1 teaspoon sea salt, to taste
½ tablespoon honey or agave syrup, to taste
2 mackerel fillets (approx. 220g/7½oz), boned, skin on

FOR THE TOPPINGS:
½ cucumber, halved lengthways, deseeded, and sliced into batons
1 small red onion, thinly sliced
115g (4oz) tinned pineapple rings or pieces
handful of fresh mint leaves, roughly torn (optional)
1 bird's-eye chilli, finely chopped (optional)

Place the noodles in a large bowl and cover with boiling water. Leave to stand for 10–15 minutes until softened, then drain and set aside until needed.

Meanwhile, heat ½ tablespoon of the vegetable oil in a large wok over a medium–high heat. Add the onion and fry for 5–6 minutes to soften, then add the chilli paste and paprika. Mix well and fry for another couple of minutes.

Now add the stock, mussel or fish sauce and tamarind to the pan, increase the heat to high and bring to the boil. Simmer for 5 minutes over a high heat, then add the lemon juice. Check the seasoning, then add salt and honey, a little at a time, until the flavours are just right. Be careful – though, it's easier to add than to take away! Set aside over very low heat for 5 minutes.

Using a sharp knife, lightly score the mackerel skin. Try not to cut all the way through into the flesh – just make a couple of slight cuts in the same direction. Place a frying pan (skillet) over a high heat and add the remaining ½ tablespoon oil. Once it's smoking hot, place the mackerel fillets, skin-side down, in the hot pan. They should make some satisfying sizzly sounds! Fry for 6 minutes, then take the pan off the heat and turn the fillets over. The other side of the fish will cook in the residual heat of the pan. Set aside for a moment.

Divide the noodles between the bowls, then layer a selection of the fresh toppings on top. Ladle over the broth to ensure the noodles are well covered. Finally, add a mackerel fillet to each bowl, crispy skin-side up. Get stuck in.

Not-your-nan's Noodle Soup

Sorry, Nan. Still love your apple pie, though!

No one makes chicken soup like your nan. But who has time to spend boiling bones to make broth? (Apart from your nan, obviously). Now you can have a big bowl of noodle-y comfort on your table in 20 minutes. Nan never needs to know. The broth is deceptively light, but it's packed with flavour thanks to the super-savoury notes from the yellow bean sauce and the nutty mushrooms.

1 teaspoon vegetable oil

300g (10½oz) minced chicken breast or chicken pieces (or use vegan mock chicken for a vegan alternative)

1 teaspoon garlic paste, or 2 garlic cloves, crushed and chopped

1 teaspoon ginger paste, or 2.5cm (1in) piece of fresh root ginger, finely chopped

1 tablespoon crushed yellow bean sauce

600ml (20fl oz) ready-made chicken bone broth, plus 600ml (20fl oz) water, or use 1.2 litres (2 pints) boiling water, if you prefer

6–7 chestnut mushrooms (approx. 170g/6oz), cleaned and sliced

100g (3½oz) dried egg noodles, or 400g (14oz) fresh egg noodles (or use rice noodles for a vegan alternative)

1 teaspoon high-quality chicken bouillon powder (or use vegan bouillon powder)

½ teaspoon light soy sauce (optional)

½ teaspoon sea salt

large pinch of white pepper

½ spring onion (scallion), finely chopped

couple of drops of cold-pressed avocado oil, flaxseed oil or sesame seed oil

Heat the oil in a deep saucepan over a medium–high heat. Add the chicken and pan-fry until it's fully cooked. If you're using a vegan alternative, just cook for 1 minute to heat through.

Increase the heat to high and add the garlic, ginger and yellow bean sauce, mixing well and cooking for another 10 seconds. Add the hot water (or stock and hot water mixture, if using) to the pan and bring to a simmer, then reduce the heat to medium–low and cook for 15 minutes.

Now add the mushrooms and noodles and simmer for a further 2 minutes (or 4 minutes if using dried noodles). Season the broth with the bouillon powder and soy sauce (if using) then with salt and pepper to taste.

Tip the soup into 2 large bowls and top with the spring onion (scallion) and a few drops of cold-pressed oil. Eat immediately and feel the world get a little cosier.

- Serves 2
- Doddle / Vegan Option / Gluten-Free Option
- Wok to wonderful in 20 minutes
- Hero ingredient: garlic (page 20)

Char Kway Teow Noodles with King Prawns & Smoked Turkey

Healthy Ho Fun Favourite

These thick, flat noodles might be called ho fun, but they're serious business in Malaysia and Singapore. Locals queue down the street to nab a table at their favourite restaurant. Traditionally cooked in pork fat, they're often served with cockles or Chinese sausage. We've kept the flavour but added some healthy tweaks. You can easily make this plant-based if you like.

400g (14oz) fresh ho fun rice noodles, or 120g (4¼oz) wide, flat dried rice noodles
3 rashers (approx. 90g/3¼oz) turkey bacon, or pancetta (if you're feeling fancy and extra flavourful), or use vegan rashers, sliced into strips
½ tablespoon vegetable oil
1 garlic clove, crushed and chopped
½ green chilli, finely chopped
1 onion, sliced
½ green bell pepper, sliced
½ red bell pepper, sliced
200g (7oz) bean sprouts
¼ teaspoon sea salt
¼ teaspoon ground white pepper
285g (10oz) cooked tail-on king prawns (jumbo shrimp), cooked chicken (or use firm tofu for a vegan alternative)
1 tablespoon mushroom or dark soy sauce
1–2 tablespoons chilli sauce, to taste
1 spring onion (scallion), finely sliced

Using your hands, separate the noodles on to a plate. Then take them for a spin in the microwave for a couple of minutes to loosen and soften them up a little (or place in a steamer for 10 minutes).

Place a large wok over a high heat and fry the turkey bacon, pancetta or vegan rashers for 1 minute, then add the oil. Stir in the garlic, green chilli, onion, red and green peppers and the bean sprouts. Mix well and season with the salt and pepper.

Next add the cooked prawns, chicken or tofu, along with the warmed noodles, soy sauce and chilli sauce. Stir well to combine and stir-fry over the same high heat for 3 minutes. To serve, tip the noodles on to a large plate, scatter with the sliced spring onion (scallion) and get stuck in – no need to queue in your kitchen!

- Serves 2 / Makes 6 small wraps
- Doddle / Vegan Option
- Wok to wonderful in 25 minutes
- Hero ingredient: sesame oil (page 20)

MR LEE'S ASIAN FAVOURITES

Duck Noodle Tortilla
Duck and roll

Here's some fusion magic for you. We take the absolute winner that is hoisin duck pancakes and give it a global twist with a stopover in Mexico City. When you combine the much-loved textures and flavours of hoisin duck with the chewy tortilla, the crunchy veggies and that sweet, tangy sauce, you get one gorgeous mouthful of two foody worlds. We're using a few crafty shortcuts to get this dish done in under 30 minutes, but as always, you won't be sacrificing flavour. This uses Mr Lee's Hoisin Sauce from the healthy store cupboard recipe section (pages 24-29). It also works great as a barbecue marinade or a salad dressing, so it's worth making a batch.

FOR THE MARINADE:

1-teaspoon garlic paste, or
   1 garlic clove, finely chopped
1 teaspoon light soy sauce
1 teaspoon dark soy sauce
1 teaspoon toasted sesame oil

250g/9oz. duck breasts, (or use mock duck
   or mock chicken, frozen or tinned)
½ red apple, core removed & skin on,
   cut into matchsticks
¼ cucumber, core removed and skin on,
   cut into matchsticks
2 small fresh tomatoes, core removed and
   cut into matchsticks
100g (3½oz) fresh thin rice noodle or fresh wheat noodle
½ teaspoon vegetable oil

2 tablespoons homemade hoisin sauce (page 25)
6 x mini soft plain tortilla

Mix together the marinade ingredients in a medium bowl. Remove the duck skin and cut the meat into strips, put it in the bowl and let it soak up that lovely sauce for 3–4 minutes.

In another medium bowl, add the prepped tomato, apple and cucumber and mix together ready for serving.

Place a wok over a high heat with the vegetable oil and then stir-fry the duck pieces for 2 minutes. Add the noodles and cook for another 2 minutes, mixing well. Set aside for serving.

Serve the tortillas slightly warmed; 20–30 seconds in a microwave or in a dry pan will get them warm and pillowy soft. Place a tortilla on a plate and spread the hoisin sauce to your liking, add some duck noodles and top with the salad. Roll, eat immediately and go on a global food tour in seconds.

Thai-style Oyster Omelette

Seafood Street-Food Superstar

You'll find this popular dish in bustling Thai city side streets, thrown together on screamingly hot street-food stoves. The salty sweet pop of the seafood and the crunchy veg make it a work of eggy brilliance. Oysters were originally a poor man's food. But If you don't want to 'shell out' for them (thank you, we're here all week!), you can easily substitute mussels or clams.

28g (1oz) fresh or dried thin rice vermicelli noodles
3 eggs
½ tablespoon tapioca starch or cornflour (corn starch)
1½ tablespoons light soy sauce (or use tamari for a gluten free option).
2 tablespoons vegetable oil
8–12 fresh, frozen or tinned oysters, raw or cooked
100g (3½oz) bean sprouts
1 spring onion (scallion), finely sliced, green and white parts separated

TO SERVE
1–2 tablespoons Mr Lee's South East Asian Hot Sauce (page 24)
small handful of fresh coriander (cilantro) leaves (optional)

Get all your prep done up front and have your serving plate and sauce ready before you start cooking. This dish moves fast and it'll be on the plate in a matter of minutes.

If you're using dried rice noodles, place them in a small pan covered with boiling water over a high heat. Boil for 2 minutes, then drain and set aside. Once cooled, cut the noodles into smaller pieces by snipping them 5 or 6 times with scissors. If you're using fresh noodles, cut them in the same way.

Beat the eggs and tapioca starch together in a small bowl, seasoning with a dash of the soy sauce.

Heat 1 tablespoon of oil in the medium wok over a high heat. Add the oysters to the pan, followed by the noodles, half the bean sprouts and the white part of the spring onion (scallion). Mix well to combine, then add the remaining soy sauce and stir-fry for 1 minute. Tip into bowl or plate, and set aside for a minute or two.

Add the remaining oil to the hot pan and pour in the beaten eggs. Using a spatula, roughly mix the egg, almost like a rough scramble, moving the cooked egg from the bottom of the pan. Give the pan a good shake, then stop moving the loose mixture around. Let the omelette take shape and start to cook through, reducing the heat to medium–high. Add the oyster mixture to cover one half of the omelette. Cook for a further minute.

Add the remaining bean sprouts on top of the oysters, and using the spatula, carefully fold the omelette to make a half moon/semi circle shape, with the bean sprouts and oyster mixture sandwiched in the middle.

Slide the omelette on to the serving plate, and drizzle with some hot sauce and a sprinkle of fresh coriander (cilantro) leaves, if you like. Sit back, breathe it in and picture yourself on the side of the Khaosan Road – hopefully staying in one of the nicer hostels.

Creamy Steak Noodles
Ditch the Chips!

Sometimes you need a regular steak fix – but it doesn't always have to come with chips! This cheeky little fusion number from Mr Lee's kitchen brings some creamy, noodle-y umami to the party. Plus, if you have one to hand, you can add a bit of theatre by serving it sizzling and smoking on a hot cast-iron serving platter. Dry ice and matching white tigers are optional.

225g–340g (8–12oz) fillet or rib-eye steak
1 teaspoon vegetable oil
2 teaspoons garlic paste, or 2–3 garlic cloves, crushed and chopped
1 banana shallot, finely diced
½ onion, sliced
½ green bell pepper, finely diced
½ red bell pepper, finely diced
½ red chilli, finely chopped
1 tablespoon Mr Lee's Healthy Mussel Sauce (page 24) or ready-made oyster sauce
½ tablespoon crushed yellow bean sauce
3 tablespoons red wine
400ml (14fl oz) boiling water
1 tablespoon cornflour (corn starch), mixed with a splash of water to make a paste
200ml (7fl oz) double (heavy) cream
350g (12oz) fresh egg noodles, or 120g (4¼oz) dried egg noodles
sea salt and freshly ground black pepper

Cast-iron platter, for serving (optional)

If you're going to Las Vegas it up with an cast-iron serving platter, place it in the oven now, on a very high heat, for 20 minutes.

Place a frying pan (skillet) over a high heat and pan-fry the steak to your liking. Once cooked, remove the steak from the pan and leave it to rest for 10 minutes.

Meanwhile, heat the oil in a medium saucepan over a high heat. Add the garlic, shallot, onion, chilli and red and green bell peppers and cook for 2 minutes. Stir in the mussel sauce, yellow bean sauce, red wine and boiling water and cook for another minute.

Next add the cornflour (corn starch) paste and bring to a simmer to thicken the sauce. Then add the cream, stir well and remove from the heat. Season with salt and pepper to taste and set aside.

If you're using dried noodles, place them in a pan of boiling water and simmer for 3 minutes until cooked, then drain. Place the frying pan you used for the steak back over a high heat and add the fresh noodles or the drained cooked ones. Cook for a few minutes until they start to get crispy.

Carefully remove the hot cast-iron serving platter from the oven (if using), and place the noodles on to the platter or in a side dish. Slice the rested steak into strips 1–2cm (½–¾in) wide and lay them on top of the noodles if you like. Pour over the sauce and serve immediately. Set off the dry ice, release the white tigers, cue laser show (optional).

- Serves 2
- Doddle / Vegan Option
- Wok to wonderful in 20 minutes
- Hero ingredients: garlic and peppercorns (page 20/21)

Filipino-Style Tangy Tomato Noodles

Thriller from Manila

This is a family favourite in the Philippines. It's a doddle to make and packs a flavourful punch. The ginger works beautifully with the chicken, and the noodles and white cabbage bring another layer of texture. The tangy, fresh tomato base reminds us of an Italian spaghetti pomodoro that had a fling in Manila.

250g (9oz) cooked chicken breast, sliced (or firm tofu, for a vegan alternative), cut into bite-sized pieces
400g (14oz) dried chow mein noodles or thick wheat noodles
1 tablespoon vegetable oil
1 tablespoon garlic paste, or 4–6 garlic cloves, finely chopped
1 teaspoon ginger paste, or 2.5cm (1in) piece of fresh root ginger, finely chopped
4 fresh tomatoes, quartered, or 16–20 cherry tomatoes, halved
200g (7oz) fresh white cabbage, finely shredded
½ teaspoon sea salt
½ teaspoon ground white pepper
1 fresh red chilli, finely sliced, to garnish (optional)

FOR THE MARINADE:
2 tablespoons Mr Lee's Healthy Mussel Sauce (page 24), or ready-made fish sauce (or Mr Lee's Vegan 'Fish' Sauce on page 25 for a vegan alternative)
2 tablespoons light soy sauce
2 tablespoons toasted sesame oil

Mix together all the marinade ingredients in a medium bowl. Add the chicken or tofu pieces and mix it all up. Set aside for a few minutes to marinate.

Half-fill a small saucepan with boiling water and place it over a high heat. Add the dried noodles and cook for 4–5 minutes, then drain and set aside.

Place a large frying pan (skillet) over a high heat and add the vegetable oil. When it's really smoking hot, add the chicken or tofu pieces. Keep the leftover marinade to add later. Stir-fry for 2 minutes over high heat.

Then add the garlic, ginger, tomatoes and cabbage, and mix well. Continue to cook for another 2–3 minutes. Season to taste with salt and pepper, then add the noodles and the remaining marinade. Mix well and stir-fry everything together for another 2 minutes.

Pile the noodle mixture on to a large serving plate and serve immediately, with some fresh chilli on the side, if you like.

- Serves 2
- A Little Effort / Vegan Option
- Wok to wonderful in 25 minutes
- Hero ingredients: garlic and peppercorns (page 20/21)

MR LEE'S ASIAN FAVOURITES

Boxing Day Chow Mein

It's a Festive Fusion Miracle!

Ditch the turkey sambo this year and give your taste buds an exotic Asian holiday.

This recipe is tailor-made for your Boxing Day challenge. Your body's still trying to digest yesterday's Christmas carnage and you have a fridge full of random leftovers to deal with. Mr Lee's has your back. This will make you feel zingy and fresh again.

240g (8½oz) cooked turkey breast, thinly sliced (or use mock turkey for a vegan alternative)
120g (4¼oz) dried chow mein noodles or thick wheat noodles
1–2 tablespoons vegetable oil
1 teaspoon garlic paste, or 1 garlic clove, crushed and finely chopped
100g (3½oz) fresh or cooked Brussels sprouts, thinly sliced
½ small carrot, thinly sliced
100g (3½oz) red cabbage, finely sliced
1 teaspoon sea salt
1 teaspoon ground white pepper
4 teaspoons cranberry sauce, to serve (optional)

FOR THE MARINADE:

1 teaspoon toasted sesame oil
2 tablespoons dark soy sauce
1 tablespoon light soy sauce
2 teaspoons classic hot English mustard

In a medium-sized bowl, mix together the marinade ingredients, then add the turkey or mock turkey pieces. Mix well and set aside for 4–5 minutes to marinate.

Place the noodles in a large bowl of boiling water and soak for 15 minutes. Once softened, drain and set aside.

Heat the oil in a large wok over a high heat. and add the vegetable oil. When it's smoking hot, carefully add the turkey/mock turkey slices to the pan and cook for 1 minute. Keep the marinade for later.

Add the garlic, sprouts, carrot and cabbage and mix well, cooking for another minute. Season with salt and white pepper to taste. Then stir in the softened noodles, and finally add the leftover marinade. Mix everything together really well to combine, stir-frying for another minute. Then pile on to a large serving plate and serve immediately, with some cranberry sauce on the side if you like – and a mince pie for dessert. It is Christmas, after all.

Singapore-style Noodles

Older Spice

Singapore is a melting pot of influences and the heart of spice trading across the southern hemisphere. You can taste that history in every mouthful of this dish. The earthy subcontinent curry spices work beautifully with the vibrant turmeric. It's a celebration of Singaporean vibrance.

125g (4½oz) dried rice vermicelli noodles
2 teaspoons vegetable oil
2 eggs, lightly beaten
4 rashers turkey bacon, sliced into small pieces
2 teaspoons garlic paste, or 4 garlic cloves, crushed and chopped
2 small onions or banana shallots, finely sliced
1 small green bell pepper, sliced
1 small red bell pepper, sliced
200g (7oz) bean sprouts
2 teaspoons mild/medium curry powder
1 teaspoon ground turmeric
225g (8oz) cooked crayfish tail without shells
1 teaspoon sea salt
1 teaspoon ground white pepper
1 large fresh chilli finely sliced, or 1 teaspoon dried chilli flakes, to taste

Place the noodles in a large bowl of boiling water and soak for 15 minutes. Once softened, drain and set aside.

Heat 1 teaspoon of the oil in a wok over a high heat. Add the beaten eggs and cook into an omelette. Once cooked through, tip on to a small plate. Once it's cool enough to handle, slice the omelette into strips and set aside for later.

Return the wok to a medium–high heat and add the remaining 1 teaspoon oil. Add the bacon pieces and fry for 1–2 minutes until lightly browned. Next add the garlic, onions, peppers and bean sprouts, and stir-fry for another 1–2 minutes.

Now add the noodles, curry powder and turmeric. Mix together so everything is well coated. Increase the heat to high and add the crayfish tails. Stir-fry for another 3 minutes, stirring continuously.

Season with salt and pepper to taste. To serve, pile the noodles high on to a large plate and top with the omelette strips. Scatter with fresh or dried chilli for an extra spicy kick. Serve immediately with an optional Singapore Sling to cool things down a bit.

School Noodle Box
Too Cool for School

School lunches can be a daily trial. You want to give them something healthy that they'll actually eat. This is a doddle to prep in advance and the sweet, moreish sauce is perfect for young palettes. Once it smothers those crunchy veggies and noodles, they'll never know it's good for them! If your kids like a little spice you can add some extra chilli.

60g (2¼oz) dried wheat noodles
10 leaves iceberg lettuce, finely sliced
¼ red bell pepper, finely sliced
½ small carrot, grated
80–100g (2¾–3½oz) cooked chicken, shredded
   (or use grilled aubergine/eggplant slices for
   a vegan alternative)
¼ teaspoon sesame seeds (optional)

FOR THE SAUCE:
½ tablespoon light soy sauce
½ tablespoon dark soy sauce
½ tablespoon no-added-sugar tomato ketchup
½ tablespoon honey (or use agave syrup for
   a vegan alternative)

Half-fill a small sauce pan with boiling water and place it over a medium heat. Add the dried noodles and boil for 4 minutes, then place them in a bowl of cold water to stop them cooking further. Set aside until needed.

In a small bowl, mix together the sauce ingredients.

Drain the noodles and tip into a large bowl. Add the shredded lettuce and half the sauce mixture, then combine well.

Place the noodle mixture into your lunch box. Add the pepper, carrot and chicken (or aubergine/eggplant). Sprinkle over the sesame seeds (all that goodness!). Pour over remaining sauce or serve in a tightly sealed jar or tub. Seal and leave in the fridge ready to take to school. The next morning, kick back, have a coffee, maybe read a newspaper. Lunch is sorted.

- Serves 2 as starter, 1 as main
- Doddle / <15 Min / Gluten-Free / Vegetarian / Vegan Option
- Wok to wonderful in 14 minutes
- Hero ingredient: peppercorns (page 24)

Mr Lee's Melty Noodle Pizza Bites

A little pizza fusion magic (sorry, can't resist a pizza pun)

This is a great, healthy alternative that uses naturally gluten-free rice noodles, but still delivers a pizza hit. The tangy hoisin and tomato base is slathered on to the crisped noodle 'pizza base', and then you can just go crazy with your toppings and finish it off with that all-important melted cheese. It's a healthy crowd-pleaser that delivers on every level.

100g (3½oz) dried rice vermicelli noodles
1 tablespoon Mr Lee's Hoisin Sauce (page 25)
1 tablespoon low-sugar tomato ketchup
½ tablespoon vegetable oil
80g (2¾oz) Cheddar cheese or Monterey Jack, grated (or use a vegan cheese)
2 fresh tomatoes, cut into 0.5–1cm (¼–½in) dice
½ small avocado, cut into 0.5–1cm (¼–½in) dice
freshly ground black pepper

Half-fill a small saucepan with boiling water and place over a medium–high heat. Add the dried noodles and boil for 3 minutes, then separate the noodles into 4 equal portions.

Mix together the hoisin sauce and ketchup in a small bowl and set aside.

Heat the oil in a large frying pan (skillet) over a high heat. Using a metal pastry ring or cookie-cutter circle, if you've got it, form the noodles into little patty shapes in the hot pan. Press down on the noodles firmly with a spatula or fish slice as they start to crisp up. Cook for 3 minutes on one side.

Carefully turn over the rice noodle bases and continue to cook on the second side while you're adding the toppings. Spoon some of the tomato-and-hoisin mixture on to each noodle patty, then top with cheese. Top the patties with tomato, and avocado pieces.

Place a large lid on top of the pan and cook for a further 2–3 minutes until the cheese has melted. Sprinkle with black pepper and serve immediately.

Noodle Box for Grown-ups

Instant Office Envy

This hot and sweet lunchtime legend will help you smash your day. Put it together with whatever you have in the fridge, but hold off on adding the warming, subtle black rice vinegar until you're ready to eat, because it'll break down the noodles. You can enjoy this cold or add boiling water to create a saucy or even soupy bowl of noodles. Kevin from Accounts will be so jealous.

60g (2¼oz) dried wheat noodles
½ tablespoon vegetable oil
2 turkey rashers (or use 2 vegan rashers
　for a vegetarian alternative)
1 egg
small handful of bean sprouts,
　or ¼ small cucumber, chopped
¼ green bell pepper, finely sliced
½ large tomato, chopped
½ spring onion (scallion), finely sliced
1 teaspoon toasted sesame seeds
fresh red chilli (optional)

FOR THE SAUCE:
½ tablespoon Chinese black rice vinegar
½ tablespoon light soy sauce
½ tablespoon dark soy sauce
½ tablespoon mirin
½ tablespoon honey, (or use agave syrup
　for a vegan alternative)
½ teaspoon dried chilli flakes

Place a small pan of boiling water over a medium heat. Add the dried noodles and boil for 4 minutes, then place them in a bowl of cold water to stop them cooking further. Set aside.

In a small bowl, mix together the sauce ingredients. Once combined, pour the sauce into a small well-sealed container. Make sure it can't leak out, or it'll be a saucy lunchtime disaster!

Heat the oil in a medium frying pan (skillet) over a medium–high heat. Break the egg into a cup and lightly whisk. Pour it into the pan and fry to make a thin omelette. Turn the omelette once to finish cooking, then transfer the cooked omelette to a chopping board and leave to cool.

Place the same pan over a high heat and add the turkey or vegan rashers. Fry for 30 seconds on each side, turning once. Then remove from the pan and place on a piece of paper towel to cool.

Roll the omelette into a cylinder shape, then slice it into finger-width strips. Slice the rashers into thin strips too.

Drain the cooked noodles well and tip them into your lunch box or jar. Now add the toppings, starting with the bean sprouts, followed by the rashers, egg, pepper and tomato. Finally sprinkle with spring onion (scallion), sesame seeds and chilli (if using). Seal and place in the fridge until ready to take to work.

To serve, add the sauce mixture to the noodles and mix well. You can enjoy it cold, or add 200ml (7fl oz) boiling water to make it saucy or 400ml (14fl oz) to make it soupy. Try to ignore the envious gaze of Kevin from Accounts as you tuck in. Maybe bring him some next time.

- Serves 2 as main (makes 12 skewers)
- A Little Effort / One-Wok Wonder / Gluten-Free Option
- Wok to wonderful in 25 minutes
- Hero ingredients: lemongrass and turmeric (page 21)

Mr Lee's Balinese-style Skewers with Peanut Satay Sauce

South East Asia on a Stick

Things on sticks are always a winner and these skewers serve up a world of fragrant South East Asian flavours, all drizzled in the super-savoury nutty satay sauce. And it's adaptable to lots of other dishes. Great as a simple stir-fry sauce with vegetables and the protein of your choice, or as a marinade or dipping sauce for simple vegetable skewers.

½ tablespoon vegetable oil
200ml (7fl oz) Mr Lee's Healthy Peanut Satay Sauce, (page 26), plus extra to serve
freshly chopped coriander (cilantro), to serve
freshly sliced red chilli, to serve

12 x 15cm (6in) bamboo skewers

FOR THE SKEWERS:
20g (¾oz) dried rice vermicelli noodles or mung bean noodles
280-300g (10oz) lean chicken or turkey mince
1 heaped teaspoon finely chopped lemongrass stalk
2 anchovies, finely chopped
1 teaspoon garlic paste, or 2 garlic cloves, crushed and chopped
½ teaspoon black pepper
1 teaspoon Mr Lee's Healthy Mussel Sauce (page 24) or ready-made fish sauce
1 teaspoon light soy sauce (or use tamari for a gluten-free option)
1 tablespoon cornflour (corn starch)
½ tablespoon peanut butter
½ teaspoon ground turmeric
1 teaspoon honey or agave syrup
½ teaspoon lemon or lime zest

FOR THE SALAD:
100g (3½oz) cucumber, cut into small dice
100g (3½oz) beetroot, cut into small dice
100g (3½oz) red onion, cut into small dice

Soak the vermicelli noodles in a bowl of boiling water for 1 minute, then drain well. Roughly chop the noodles and place them in a large mixing bowl with all the other skewer ingredients. Using your hands (you can wear food-safe gloves if you like), combine everything together, mixing well. Wet your hands and shape the mixture into 12 small sausage shapes, each around 5cm (2in) long. Thread each one on to a bamboo skewer, to make 12 skewers. Set aside in fridge for 10-15 minutes if you have time.

Heat the oil in a large frying pan (skillet) over a medium-high heat. Add the skewers and fry for 2 minutes on each side, then reduce the heat to low and cook for a further 1 minute on one side only. Remove the skewers from the pan and lay on a plate lined with paper towel to drain any excess oil.

Mix together the salad ingredients and place on a large serving platter (or divide between plates). Lay the skewers on top and drizzle the skewers with the peanut satay sauce (warmed through if you prefer). Scatter over a few fresh coriander (cilantro) leaves and some fresh red chilli slices. Serve immediately, with extra satay sauce on the side.

Mr Lee's Spiced Prawn Toastie-Samosa

Marvellously Moreish

We take two of the most moreish starters from Indian and Chinese cookery and squish them together into one ('squish' is a cheffy term). This is actually made with bread instead of pastry, so it's much easier to prepare. Plus the rich tomatoey dip is a doddle to make, can be done in advance and keeps in the fridge for up to a week.

---

1 tablespoon dried mung bean noodles
   or rice vermicelli noodles
160g (5½oz) raw prawns (shrimp),
   peeled and de-veined, finely diced
pinch of sea salt
pinch of ground white pepper
½ teaspoon toasted sesame oil
1 teaspoon cornflour (corn starch)
½ teaspoon medium curry powder
½ teaspoon garam masala
6 slices of fresh bread, white or brown
1 egg
1 tablespoon vegetable oil

FOR THE DIPPING SAUCE:
1 teaspoon olive oil
1 teaspoon garlic paste, or use 2 garlic cloves,
   crushed and finely chopped
1 tablespoon no-added-sugar tomato ketchup
¼ tablespoon chilli flakes
½ tablespoon freshly chopped coriander (cilantro)
   or mint

To make the sauce, heat the 1 teaspoon olive oil in a small frying pan (skillet) over a high heat. Add the garlic and fry for 10 seconds, then transfer the garlic to a small mixing bowl. Add the remaining sauce ingredients and mix well. Set aside.

Place the dried noodles in a bowl of boiling water, then leave to stand for 5 minutes until soft. Drain and leave to dry, then cut the noodles into smaller pieces with scissors.

Place the diced prawn (shrimp) meat in a small bowl. Add the salt, pepper, sesame oil and cornflour (corn starch), mixing well. Stir in the curry powder and garam masala, along with the noodles. Stir well to combine and set aside.

Remove the crusts of the bread to make a perfect square shape. Then lightly beat the egg in a small cup, ready to seal the edges. Using a rolling pin, flatten the bread slices to make them thinner and pastry-like.

Divide the filling into six portions. Place each portion in the centre of a bread slice. Brush the edges of the bread with egg, then fold diagonally to form a triangle shape, enclosing the filling. Use the back of a butter knife to seal the edges of the bread, forming a sealed triangle. Repeat to fill and seal the other slices, to make 6 filled toasties.

Place a large frying pan over a high heat and add the vegetable oil. Place three toasties into the pan and fry for 3 minutes on each side, until golden brown and crisp all over. Lay the cooked toasties on a plate lined with paper towel, to drain any excess oil.

Repeat with the final batch, adding more oil as necessary. Once all cooked, divide amongst serving plates or arrange on a sharing platter with a lovely pot of the spicy tomato dip. Serve immediately, eat, then instantly go and make a second batch...or at least that tends to be how it works when we make it.

- Serves 2
- Doddle / <15 Min / One-Wok Wonder
- Wok to wonderful in 12 minutes
- Hero ingredient: anchovies (page 23)

Burmese-style Noodles with Crayfish (Khao-swe Kyaw)

Burma Brings it All

This stir-fry has it all: nutty, savoury and a little bit spicy. Plus the fast-fried crayfish and cabbage bring some sweetness. Khao-swe is Burmese for noodle, and Kyaw simply means fried. We've kept it simple by just using crayfish tails, but you can add whatever cooked meat or seafood you have in the fridge, or use tofu or mock chicken for a vegan alternative.

120g (4¼oz) dried egg noodles, or 350g (12oz) fresh wheat noodles
1 tablespoon vegetable oil
1 anchovy, finely chopped
2 teaspoons garlic paste, or 4 garlic cloves, crushed and chopped
¼ white cabbage (approx. 285g/10z, finely sliced
140g (5oz) crayfish tails or cooked prawns (shrimp)
6 Asian shallots (the tiny ones) or 1 banana shallot, finely diced
2 small green chillies, finely diced, or ½ teaspoon dried chilli flakes
½ red pepper, sliced
1 teaspoon ground turmeric
1 teaspoon toasted sesame seeds
1½ tablespoons light soy sauce
handful of fresh coriander (cilantro), to garnish
Mr Lee's South East Asian Hot Sauce (page 24), to serve

Place the noodles in a large bowl and cover with boiling water. Leave to sit for 3 minutes, then drain and rinse with cold water. Leave to dry in a colander or sieve.

Place a large wok over a high heat and the oil, followed by the anchovy, garlic and cabbage. Stir-fry for 1 minute, then add the crayfish or prawns (shrimp), shallots, chillies, red bell pepper, turmeric and sesame seeds. Fry for another 30 seconds, then add the soy sauce. Mix well and cook for another 2 minutes.

Pile the noodles on to a large serving plate and scatter with fresh coriander (cilantro). Serve immediately, with South East Asian hot sauce on the side.

● Serves 2 as a starter
or light meal

● Doddle / <15 Min /
Gluten-Free Option

● Wok to wonderful in
12 minutes

Hero ingredients: garlic
and ginger (page 20/22)

Singapore-style Chilli Crab

Messy memories of Singapore

This dish instantly takes us back to our childhoods. Perched high on a chair way too big for us on a muggy day in downtown Singapore, tying on a bib and diving into this saucy, spicy, crabby mess. And it was really messy. Well, maybe we were messy, too – it probably wasn't entirely the crab's fault.

60g (2¼oz) dried rice vermicelli noodles,
or use fresh if you prefer

½ tablespoon vegetable oil

1 teaspoon crushed garlic

1 teaspoon ground ginger

1 large fresh red chilli, finely chopped

4 small cherry tomatoes, finely diced

1 teaspoon fermented soy bean paste, crushed yellow
bean sauce, ready-made fish sauce or soy sauce

145–200g (5–7oz) fresh crab meat, with a mixture
of white and brown meat, or use tinned white meat

1 egg, beaten

2–3 teaspoons water

1 teaspoon honey or agave syrup

¼ teaspoon ground white pepper

1 teaspoon rice vinegar

½ spring onion (scallion), green part only,
finely sliced, to garnish

Place the dried vermicelli noodles in a saucepan of boiling water over a medium–high heat. Simmer for 3–4 minutes until soft, then drain and set aside.

Heat the oil in a wok over a high heat and add the garlic, ginger, chilli and tomatoes. Stir-fry for 5 seconds, then pour in the egg, fermented soybean paste, crushed yellow bean sauce, fish sauce or soy sauce and keep stirring, over a very high heat, for 30-45 seconds, so the egg is half cooked.

Add the crab-mixture, along with the water, honey and white pepper (and the fresh noodles if using). Stir-fry for another minute or so over a high heat, until everything is heated through. Remove the pan from the heat.

Now add the rice vinegar and mix everything well. Adjust to taste, adding a little more vinegar if you prefer a sour-spicy flavour.

Place the rice noodles on a serving plate and pour the crab meat on top. Finish with a garnish of spring onion (scallion) and serve with a large fresh salad on the side.

As you'd expect from one of the world's oldest civilisations, China has a rich and eclectic food history. Some of your favourite takeaway treats were actually created in the vast palaces of Imperial dynasties hundreds of years ago. With over 1,000 types of noodles, the sheer variety of techniques and ingredients is astonishing. This whole book could be just about Chinese cuisine and we'd still just be scratching the noodle surface.

There's something about Chinese food that hits the spot like nothing else. In this section, we'll take you on a journey of noodle-y discovery from the Northern Chinese provinces to the tongue-tingling Sichuan region, taking in Shanghai, Macau, and Hong Kong for some street-food and restaurant-style treats.

We've got the stone-cold classics that everyone loves, like chow-mein. Because sometimes it just has to be soft noodles, crunchy beansprouts and that delicate balance of light and dark soy from this global winner. And traditional Yum Cha dishes aka dim sum, where some recipes are so fast and easy, we are talking prep to plate faster than you can ring your local takeaway. Plus some real showstoppers if you want to impress your friends.

All of these recipes have been given the Mr Lee's treatment, so you count on them to be super-healthy, super easy and super-tasty! The recipes are simpler, healthier but still a gorgeous Mr Lee's spin on the classic. We ditch the nasties like sugar in favour of healthy alternatives, and harness the healthy protein options.

2

Chinese

- Serves 2
- Showing Off / Vegan Option
- Wok to wonderful in 20 minutes
- Hero ingredients: garlic and ginger (page 20/22)

Dan Dan Noodle Soup with Lamb

Bring on the Tingle

A 'dan dan' is the pole that noodle sellers use to carry the baskets of fresh noodles and sauce, with one at either end. The star is Sichuan chilli bean paste, or toban djan (see page 17) but you can use other chilli pastes if you can't get your hands on it. Combined with the Sichuan peppercorns, you get a lip-tingling intensity. You can also try it as a stir-fry dish by omitting the stock water, and using fresh noodles.

½ tablespoon vegetable oil

230g (8¼oz) minced (ground) lamb
(or frozen vegan mince and ¼ tsp yeast extract for a vegan alternative)

2 teaspoons garlic paste, or 3–4 garlic cloves, crushed and chopped

1 tablespoon ginger paste or 5cm (2in) piece of fresh root ginger, chopped

1 carrot, finely diced

1 large onion, finely diced

120g (4¼oz) dried wheat noodles

1 spring onion (scallion), finely sliced, to garnish

FOR THE SOUP:

600ml (20fl oz) boiling water, or ready-made fresh vegetable stock

1 tablespoon crushed yellow bean sauce, or brown or red miso paste

1 tablespoon chilli bean paste, or 1 teaspoon any hot chilli paste

2 teaspoons crunchy peanut butter

½ teaspoon ground Sichuan peppercorns

1 tablespoon toasted sesame oil

Prepare the soup mixture by mixing all the ingredients together in a large bowl or jug, then set aside until needed.

Heat the oil in a large wok over a high heat. Throw in the minced lamb (or vegan mince) and brown for a few seconds. Then add the garlic, ginger, carrot and onion and cook for another 2 minutes, stirring continuously. Your kitchen should smell amazing at this stage, so take a second, stop and breathe it in. But don't take all day, we're on a schedule!

Next pour the soup mixture into the pan and mix well, simmering for another 3 minutes.

Now it's noodle time. Put the noodles in a saucepan and cover with boiling water. Boil for 3 minutes, then drain. Divide your hot noodles between 2 serving bowls and pour over the soupy mixture. Sprinkle over the chopped spring onion (scallion). Strap in your taste buds: you'll never forget your first Dan Dan Noodle Soup.

- Serves 2
- Doddle / <15 Min / One-Wok Wonder / Vegan Option
- Wok to wonderful in 15 minutes
- Hero ingredient: garlic (page 20)

Shanghai 'Yum Cha' Noodles with Chicken & Pak Choi

Bye-bye Soggy leftover Chicken Sandwiches

This is a great way to give leftover roast chicken a tingly makeover. In Southern China, locals get together for tea, dumplings and a steaming bowl of noodles in one of the many Yum Cha restaurants. It's kind of like going for afternoon tea, Shanghai-style. But anytime can be Yum Cha time: morning, afternoon, when you get home from the pub. If you can't get Shanghai noodles use udon.

400g (14oz) fresh Shanghai or udon noodles
½ tablespoon vegetable oil
1 teaspoon garlic paste, or 2 small garlic cloves, crushed and chopped
¼ small white cabbage (approx. 150g/5½oz), finely sliced
1 carrot, finely sliced
200g (7oz) fresh pak choi (bok choy), roughly chopped into bite-sized pieces
190g (6¾oz) roasted or cooked chicken, cut into thin (really thin!) slices (or use mock chicken or tofu for a vegan alternative)
¼ teaspoon sea salt
¼ teaspoon ground black pepper

FOR THE STIR-FRY SAUCE:
1 tablespoon dark soy sauce
1 tablespoon toasted sesame oil

Put the noodles in a large bowl or saucepan and cover with boiling water. Stir for 20 seconds, then drain well and set aside.

For the sauce, mix together the soy sauce and sesame oil in a small cup or bowl and set aside until needed.

Heat the oil in a large wok and place it over a smoking-hot high heat. And we do mean smoking! Add the garlic, cabbage, carrot and pak choi (bok choy), along with the noodles and chicken (or mock chicken/tofu).

Pour over the sauce, season with salt and pepper and continue stirring for 3 minutes. Pour the noodles directly on to two plates and dive in while everything is still sizzling.

Hot & Dry Street Food Noodles

Feel-good-taste-good Pot Noodle

If you're after something quick and tangy to get your taste buds rocking, this is the one. Earthy chilli, sour vinegar and sharp garlic all together? Noodle-nom. It's a bit like a Pot Noodle, but the Mr Lee's way: healthy, full of flavour and no nasties. Have it as a snack or with stir-fried veg. The star ingredient is black vinegar, rice vinegar's chilled out, mellow cousin.

60–75g (2–2¾oz) dried flat wheat noodles, 3mm (⅛in) wide

FOR THE SAUCE:
1 tablespoon garlic paste, or 3 garlic cloves, crushed and finely chopped
1 tablespoon light soy sauce
1 tablespoon black vinegar, or rice vinegar
1 spring onion (scallion), green part only, finely chopped
¼–1 large fresh red chilli, to taste

Place all the sauce ingredients in a small bowl and mix them together.

Half-fill a small saucepan with boiling water and place over a high heat. Add the dried noodles, bring to the boil and simmer for 2 minutes, then drain. Mix the noodles with the sauce and erm … that's it really. Serve! Told you it was quick.

- Serves 2
- Showing Off
- Wok to wonderful in 30 minutes
- Hero ingredients: ginger and broccoli (page 22/23)

Hong Kong Street Beef
A Big Beefy Hug

Mr Lee's Hong Kong Street Beef noodle pot is a customer favourite, so we just had to adapt it for our very first cookbook. The richly flavoured and aromatic soup base, combined with the savoury hit of the steak, wraps you in a warm, beefy blanket of contentment. It's the best kind of comfort food: Tastes like it took hours, but ready in minutes. Winner!

1 tablespoon crushed yellow bean sauce
1 teaspoon toasted sesame oil
½ tablespoon vegetable oil
250g (9oz) rib-eye steak, or use sirloin/ porterhouse if you prefer
85g (3oz) sprouting broccoli, or use regular broccoli cut into bite-sized pieces
120g (4¼oz) dried thin wheat noodles (or use thin rice noodles for a gluten-free alternative)

FOR THE SOUP:
230g (8¼oz) lean minced (ground) beef, or substitute
900ml (1½ pints) of ready-made fresh beef stock
2 small onions, finely diced
2 whole star anise
1 large black cardamom pod
½ teaspoon Chinese five-spice powder
1 teaspoon ginger paste, or 2.5cm (1 inch) piece of fresh root ginger, finely chopped
1 teaspoon garlic paste, or 2 garlic cloves, crushed and chopped
½ teaspoon sea salt, or to taste
½ teaspoon finely ground black pepper
1 tablespoon crushed yellow bean sauce
900ml (1½ pints) boiling water (if not using stock)

FOR THE GARNISH:
1 spring onion (scallion), finely sliced
handful of fresh coriander (cilantro), roughly torn (optional)
2 tablespoons chilli oil (optional)

Heat a medium saucepan over a medium–high heat and brown the minced beef (if using). Then add all the other soup ingredients except the water or stock. Keep stirring for 2–3 minutes, then add the water (or stock, if using). Cover the pan with a lid and leave all those lovely flavours to simmer and intensify over a low heat for 20 minutes.

Meanwhile, mix together the yellow bean sauce and toasted sesame oil on a plate. Now it's steak time! Put the steak on the plate and really rub the marinade all over, then set it aside for a few minutes.

Heat a wok over a high heat and add the vegetable oil. Pan-fry the steak for about 3 minutes on each side. This will cook it medium – but it's your steak, so cook it how you like. If you want it a bit pinker, then cook it for up to 2 minutes each side. The super-high heat will seal the meat and keep it nice and succulent. As soon as the steak is cooked to your liking, put it on a chopping board, cover it with foil and let it rest for a bit.

Place another medium saucepan on the hob and half-fill with boiling water. Add the broccoli and boil for 2 minutes, then add the dried noodles and simmer for another minute. Drain and divide the broccoli and noodles between two large, deep soup bowls.

Using a fine sieve, strain the soup broth as you pour it over the noodles in each bowl, discarding the aromatics. Slice the steak into strips, then layer on top of the noodle soup. Garnish with spring onion (scallion) and fresh coriander (cilantro). Serve with a small pot of red chilli oil on the side for drizzling, and you're good to go.

Proper Chow Mein

Like a Takeaway – But a Squillion Times Better.

We've taken this giant of the takeaway menu and given it some Mr Lee's love, so it's fast, healthy, tasty and has none of that MSG stuff. We're going for a classic Hong Kong-style, soy sauce chow mein, which is typically for breakfast or afternoon tea. You can also make it a 'Special Chow Mein' if you're feeling fancy (top hats and ball gowns are optional).

120g (4¼oz) dried thick or thin egg noodles
  (or use egg-free yellow noodles)
1 tablespoon vegetable oil
½ teaspoon garlic paste, or 1 small garlic clove,
  crushed and finely chopped
1 tablespoon light soy sauce
½ tablespoon dark soy sauce
¼ teaspoon ground white pepper
200g (7oz) bean sprouts
few drops of toasted sesame oil

TO MAKE SPECIAL CHOW MEIN VERSION (OPTIONAL):
125g (4½oz) cooked chicken (or use mock chicken
  for a vegan alternative), roughly chopped into
  bite-sized pieces – or you can use any leftover
  cooked meats or mock meat
125g (4½oz) cooked crayfish tails or prawns (or use
  150g/5½oz oyster mushrooms for a vegan alternative)

Put the noodles in a large bowl and cover with boiling water. Leave to sit for 3 minutes, then drain and rinse with cold water. Leave to dry in a colander or sieve.

Heat the oil in a wok over a high heat, then add the garlic and drained noodles. Stir-fry for 2 minutes, mixing well. Add the dark and light soy sauce, along with the white pepper and beansprouts, and keep mixing for a minute. Finally add the sesame oil, mix again, then pile the noodles high on to a large serving plate. Serve immediately. This can be served as a main course for two people, or as a sharing plate so everyone can dive in.

To make the Special Chow Mein version:

To glam this up into a Special Chow Mein, just follow the method above, and add the cooked chicken and crayfish or prawns (or the mock chicken and mushrooms) at the same time as the beansprouts. Stir-fry on a very high heat for an extra minute, mix it all up and you have a fancy Special Chow Mein.

- Serves 2
- Doddle / <15 Min / Gluten-Free / Vegan
- Wok to wonderful in 15 minutes
- Hero ingredient: peppercorns (page 24)

Sichuan Hot & Sour Sweet Potato Noodle Soup (Suan La Fen)

Tingle-Lipping-Good

You can enjoy this Sichuan-pepper- lip-tingler on pretty much every street corner in Sichuan China. Once your taste buds tango with this bad boy, you'll be a convert for life. The slippery and slightly chewy sweet potato noodles originate from Korea, but often appear in both Korean and Chinese cooking. Plus, in true Mr Lee's style, this dish is easy, healthy and quick.

200g (7oz) dried sweet potato noodles

FOR THE SEASONING MIX:

1 teaspoon ground Sichuan peppercorns

1 teaspoon Chinese five-spice powder

2 tablespoons Mr Lee's Red Chilli Oil (page 29) or use ready-made Chinese-style red chilli oil

4 tablespoons Chinese black rice vinegar, or clear rice vinegar

2 tablespoons light soy sauce (or use tamari for gluten free)

1–2 teaspoons toasted sesame oil

½ –1 teaspoon sea salt, to taste

FOR THE SOUP:

1 tablespoon peanut, groundnut oil or vegetable oil

2 teaspoons garlic paste, or 4 garlic cloves, crushed and finely chopped

1–2 spring onions (scallions), finely sliced

few sprigs of fresh coriander (cilantro), plus extra to serve

2 tablespoons roasted peanuts, preferably red-skinned

½ fresh red chilli, finely chopped (optional, but a must if you like it spicy)

Cook the noodles according to the instructions, then drain. Meanwhile, mix together the ingredients for the seasoning mix and divide between 2 serving bowls.

Heat the oil in a wok over high heat and add the crushed garlic, stirring for a few minutes. Then divide the hot garlic-and-oil mixture between the two serving bowls and mix it all up with the seasoning mix. Throw the spring onions (scallions) and coriander (cilantro) into the bowls.

Put the drained noodles on top of the spice mixture and top up with enough freshly boiled water to just cover the noodles. Stir it up to combine all of the flavours, then top with the roasted peanuts and chillies and serve.

Holy Shiitake Mushrooms with Fresh Noodles!

The Umami Superhero

When you're after an intense umami hit, you can't get better than a shiitake mushroom. This Cantonese dish packs a super-savoury punch and is so quick and easy. The noodles are the bouncy, oily type often called 'dan dan', but they can be substituted for dried wheat noodles.

1 tablespoon vegetable oil

1 teaspoon garlic paste, or 2 garlic cloves, crushed and finely chopped

1 carrot, peeled and sliced into 5cm (2in) batons

1 red onion, thickly sliced

2 celery stalks, peeled and sliced into thin 5cm (2in) batons

120g (4¼oz) fresh shiitake mushrooms, or 30g (1oz) dried, soaked according to packet instructions

55g (2oz) mangetout (snow peas) or green beans

¼ teaspoon sea salt

¼ teaspoon ground white pepper

400g (14oz) fresh dan dan noodles, or fresh rice vermicelli for vegan option

FOR THE STIR-FRY SAUCE:

½ tablespoon light soy sauce

1 tablespoon dark soy sauce

1 teaspoon toasted sesame oil

Heat the oil in a wok over a high heat. Add the garlic, onion, carrot, celery, mushrooms and mangetout (snow peas) or green beans and stir-fry for a couple of minutes, mixing well. Season with the salt and pepper, then add your noodles and the stir-fry sauce ingredients. Toss it all together over a high heat for 3 minutes so it's nicely coated.

Pile the noodles high on a large serving plate. Serve immediately for the mushroom lover(s) in your life.

- Serves 2
- Showing Off / Vegan Option
- Wok to wonderful in 25 minutes
- Hero ingredient: peppers (page 23)

Street-market-style Pork

Pure Porky Perfection

This is proper street-food cooking. Super-simple and flavourful, you'll find this dish all over China. The sweetness of the carrots is perfectly balanced by the earthy celery, while the hoisin and pork give you that famous sweet–savouriness. It uses thick, satisfying, udon noodles with lots of texture. You can use fresh wheat noodles or even thick pasta, like tagliatelle, if you like.

250g (9oz) pork fillet, thinly sliced (or use fresh firm tofu, cut into 0.5cm/¼in slices, for a vegan alternative)
400g (14oz) fresh udon noodles, or use fresh thick wheat noodles or tagliatelle pasta (check pasta is egg-free for vegan option)
½ tablespoon vegetable oil
¼ small white cabbage, finely sliced
½ red pepper, cut into 0.5cm (¼in) slices
4 baby leeks, or use 1 large leek (approx. 400g/14oz)

FOR THE MARINADE:
2 tablespoons toasted sesame oil
1 tablespoon light soy sauce
½ teaspoon sea salt
½ teaspoon ground black pepper

FOR THE STIR-FRY SAUCE:
1 tablespoon light soy sauce
1 tablespoon dark soy sauce
1 tablespoon Mr Lee's Hoisin Sauce (page 25)
1 teaspoon toasted sesame oil

In a large bowl, mix together the marinade ingredients. Add the pork (or tofu) and stir, then set aside for 5 minutes to soak up the flavours.

Meanwhile, put the noodles in a saucepan over a medium heat and cover with boiling water. Mix well, allow to boil for 10 seconds, then drain immediately. Set aside.

In a small cup or bowl, mix together the stir-fry sauce ingredients and set aside until needed.

Place a large wok over a high heat and add the vegetable oil. Add the marinated pork (or tofu) slices to the pan, keeping any leftover marinade in the bowl, and stir well. Cook for nearly 1 minute, stirring constantly so it doesn't stick to the pan. Then add the cabbage, pepper and leeks, along with the stir-fry sauce mixture, and cook for another minute.

Finally, add the noodles, along with any leftover marinade. Stir-fry for another minute, then serve immediately.

- Serves 2
- A Little Effort
- Wok to wonderful in 30 minutes
- Hero ingredient: miso (page 21)

CHINESE

Marco Polo Noodles: Chinese Spaghetti with Beef Fillet

An East meets West Love-in

Italian-style pasta is pretty popular in China, and it's rumoured that Marco Polo introduced the idea of noodles to Italy, bringing them back from his travels. But for the sake of world noodle peace, let's say we all invented it. This is a modern take on a classic Chinese family dish. It's a rich, comforting bowl of loveliness.

225g (8oz) beef fillet (tenderloin) or rump (sirloin),
   sliced into strips
pinch of sea salt
1½ tablespoons vegetable oil, plus a splash for the pasta
120g (4¼oz) dried Italian-style spaghetti
1 teaspoon garlic paste, or 2 garlic cloves,
   crushed and finely chopped
100g (3½oz) bean sprouts
2 spring onions (scallions), finely sliced
½ tablespoon dark soy sauce
½ tablespoon light soy sauce
1 teaspoon honey or agave syrup
few drops of toasted sesame oil

FOR THE MARINADE:
1 tablespoon brown miso paste or light soy sauce
large pinch of ground white pepper
½ tablespoon cornflour (corn starch)
½ tablespoon honey or agave syrup
few drops of toasted sesame oil

Mix together all of the marinade ingredients in a medium bowl. Add the beef strips and give it all a really good mix. Put it aside for 10–15 minutes so the flavours can get to know each other.

Meanwhile, fill a large, deep saucepan with water. Add a pinch of salt and a splash of vegetable oil and place the pan over a high heat. Add the spaghetti to the boiling water and cook according to the packet instructions (usually about 8–10 minutes). Once cooked, drain the spaghetti and leave it to cool for 10 minutes.

When you're ready to cook, place a wok over a smoking-hot high heat and add 1 tablespoon of the vegetable oil. Once it's hot, add the beef strips and stir-fry to taste. How you like your steak cooked is personal – you do you. You can test how well the steak is cooked by pressing down on it with your forefinger. The firmer the feel of the steak, the more well-done it is. If it feels like the middle of your cheek, that's rare. The end of your chin is about medium. The end of your something is well-done. Big toe? Haven't a clue. Place the cooked beef strips on a board and cover with foil to rest for a few minutes.

Stick the pan back over a high heat. Add the remaining ½ tablespoon vegetable oil and stir-fry the garlic and bean sprouts for 20–30 seconds. Then add the cooked spaghetti, along with the spring onions (scallions), dark soy, light soy, honey or agave and sesame oil. Mix it up and stir-fry for 1 minute more. Then remove from the heat, add the beef and serve immediately.

- Serves 2 as
  a main course
- Showing Off/
  One-Wok Wonder /
  Vegetarian Option
- Wok to wonderful in
  30 minutes
- Hero ingredients: squid
  and broccoli (page 22/23)

Squid with Crispy Noodles and Sprouting Broccoli

Crispy-squidly-noodley-nom

Crispy noodles, fast-fried squid and super-healthy broccoli. It's a winner. If you're looking for something a bit different that everyone will love, get your crisp on. You can also lux this dish up with lobster, which you can easily buy from the supermarket these days, either frozen or fresh. If you're after a veggie option, try heart of palm instead.

85g (3oz) dried thin egg or wheat noodles

1½ tablespoons vegetable oil

1 squid (approx. 250g/9oz), cleaned, fresh or frozen; or use uncooked calamari rings (use 220g/8oz tinned heart of palm, rinse & slice into rings or batons)

1 teaspoon garlic paste, or 2 garlic cloves, crushed and chopped

½ small red onion, sliced

85g (3oz) sprouting broccoli, or use regular broccoli cut into bite-sized pieces

FOR THE SAUCE:

270ml (9fl oz) cold water

½ tablespoon cornflour (corn starch), or potato starch

1 teaspoon mirin

1 teaspoon drinking sake

1 teaspoon Mr Lee's Healthy Mussel Sauce (page 24) or use ready-made fish sauce (or use Mr Lee's Vegan 'Fish' Sauce, page 25, for a vegetarian alternative)

1 teaspoon light soy sauce

1 teaspoon crushed yellow bean sauce

1 teaspoon sesame oil

Half-fill a medium-sized deep saucepan with boiling water and place over a high heat. Add the dried noodles and cook for 1 minute 30 seconds, then drain and leave to dry in a colander or sieve for a couple of minutes.

Heat 1 tablespoon of the oil in a wok over a high heat and add the drained noodles, covering the bottom of the pan with them. Now, let's talk wok skills. The key is to get a good balance of crispy and soft bits. You'll need to do a bit of shaking, tossing and turning, but also leave them alone every now and again so they can crisp up. Throw in some dance moves if you've got an audience. It should take about 10 minutes for most of the noodles to get nice and crispy. Once the noodles are crispy, tip them on to a large serving plate. Using a large pair of scissors, snip at the noodles, making 5 or 6 cuts across them. Set aside.

In a small bowl, mix together the cornflour (corn starch) or potato starch and water to make a loose paste. Then add all the other sauce ingredients and mix well. Set aside.

Now it's time for the squid. Cut it in half and flatten it on to the chopping board, with the outside facing down. Score the inside vertically on both pieces, cutting about halfway through. Then dice the squid halves into bite-sized pieces. If using squid rings/calamari, you can simply leave the rings whole, or cut them in half.

Using the same wok as before, add the remaining ½ tablespoon vegetable oil, along with the garlic, onion and broccoli, and place over a smoking-hot high heat. Stir-fry continuously for 2 minutes, then add the squid pieces (or palm heart pieces if using) and mix well, cooking for another minute. Pour the sauce into the wok and cook the whole mixture for about 1–2 minutes, constantly mixing and shaking. Then pour the whole lot over the crispy noodles on the serving plate. Serve immediately. Stand back, take the applause, tell them it was nothing.

Punchy Pineapple Chicken

If You Like Pina Coladas … and, erm, Noodles

You'll find pineapple punching up stir-fries all over South East Asia. This Mr Lee's version mixes it up with more flavours and noodles. The sweet pineapple combined with the spicy chilli tastes a bit like a sweet and sour, but it's a flavour all of its own. Use fresh or tinned pineapple, and the chicken can easily be substituted for mock chicken or tofu.

1½ tablespoons light soy sauce

1 teaspoon toasted sesame oil

190g (6¾oz) chicken breast (or use firm tofu or mock chicken for a vegan alternative), cut into bite-sized pieces

100g (3½oz) dried thin or thick yellow noodles, or any dried wheat noodle

1 tablespoon vegetable oil

2 small red or brown onions, thinly sliced

1 tablespoon chopped leek, green part only

120g (4¼oz) pineapple, fresh or tinned, cut into 2.5cm (1in) pieces

1 fresh red chilli, finely chopped, to taste

¼ teaspoon salt, to taste

In a medium bowl, mix together the soy sauce and sesame oil. Add the chicken (or tofu/mock chicken), mix it all up and set aside for 5 minutes.

Meanwhile, put the noodles in a large bowl and cover with boiling water. Leave to sit for 7 minutes, then drain and rinse with cold water. Leave to dry in a colander or sieve.

Heat the vegetable oil in a wok over a high heat. Add the marinated chicken (or tofu/mock chicken), along with the onions, and stir-fry for 2 minutes. Then add the leek, pineapple and chilli. Mix well, then add the noodles and stir-fry for another minute or two.

Season to taste with salt if needed. Serve immediately, with optional pina coladas. And then maybe go for a walk in the rain…OK, we'll stop now.

- Serves 1
- Doddle / <15 Min / Vegan Option / Gluten-Free Option
- Wok to wonderful in 15 minutes
- Hero ingredient: shiitake mushrooms (page 22)

Ants on a Tree (Minced Pork with Mung Bean Noodles in a Spicy Sauce)

Does Not Contains Ants

Weird name, amazing porky flavours. This traditional Sichuan dish is named after the little meaty pieces of pork that look like ants climbing a noodle tree. The delicate spicing goes brilliantly with the mushrooms and the deep savoury porky-ness. Ants on a Tree is usually served as a sharing dish, but we don't like sharing, so we've adapted it for one.

45g (1½oz) dried mung bean noodles

½ tablespoon peanut oil or vegetable oil

85g (3oz) minced (ground) pork (or use ½ large aubergine/eggplant, finely diced into 1cm/½in pieces, for a vegan alternative)

¼ red onion, finely diced

1 teaspoon garlic paste, or 1 garlic clove, crushed finely chopped

3 large fresh shiitake mushrooms

2 tablespoons sake

1 tablespoon light soy sauce (or use tamari for a gluten-free alternative)

½ tablespoon chilli bean paste (toban djan), or ½ teaspoon any hot chilli paste

¼ spring onion (scallion), finely sliced, to garnish

Half-fill a small saucepan with boiling water and place over a high heat. Once it's boiling, add the noodles and reduce the heat slightly. Simmer for 2–3 minutes, then drain and set aside.

Place a large wok over a high heat and add the peanut or vegetable oil, followed by the pork mince (or aubergine/eggplant). Brown for 1 minute, then add the onion, garlic and mushrooms. Continue to stir-fry for another 2 minutes.

Now add the sake, soy sauce and chilli bean paste or chilli paste. Give it all a good stir, then add 3–6 tablespoons of water: you want the mixture to be dry, but you don't want it to catch on the bottom of the wok. So you have to watch it like a hungry hawk! Start by adding 3 tablespoons of water, and add more if you need to.

Remove the pan from the heat and add the drained noodles. Mix it all up so the noodles are covered in the sauce, then serve in a large bowl, scattering the spring onion (scallion) over the top. If you're feeling arty, you can use serving tongs to twist the noodles on top of the sauce to make it look like the traditional Ants on a Tree.

- Serves 2
- Doddle / <15 Min
- Wok to wonderful in 15 minutes
- Hero ingredient: miso (page 21)

Macau Street-food Curry Noodle Soup with Beef

Kapow from Macau

This aromatic soup is an intensely comforting bowl of loveliness that you'll often find while wandering the streets of Macau. One mouthful, and KAPOW! Instant flavour hit. Typically, you'd have to spend hours slow-cooking the broth. But we've adapted it to be cooked in a fraction of the time while still packing a flavourful punch.

250g (9oz) beef fillet (tenderloin), thinly sliced
1 tablespoon vegetable oil
1 onion, finely diced

FOR THE MARINADE:
1 teaspoon light soy sauce
½ teaspoon dark soy sauce
½ tablespoon toasted sesame oil
1 teaspoon cornflour (corn starch) or potato starch

FOR THE NOODLE SOUP BASE:
120g (4¼oz) dried thin wheat noodles
800ml (1½ pints) fresh beef stock, or use boiling water
1 tablespoon red or brown miso
½ tablespoon garam masala
1 tablespoon medium–hot curry powder
1 tablespoon light soy sauce

TO GARNISH:
fresh red chilli, cut into julienne strips (optional)
handful of fresh coriander (cilantro),
   finely chopped (optional)

In a medium bowl, mix together the marinade ingredients. Add the beef strips and stir to combine, then set aside for 5 minutes.

In a large, deep saucepan, mix together all the noodle soup base ingredients, except the noodles, and place over a high heat. Bring to simmer and add the noodles, boiling on medium heat for 3 minutes. Drain in a sieve or colander and set aside for a few minutes.

Heat a medium wok over a high heat and add the vegetable oil. Add the marinated beef and sizzle for about 1 minute, then add the onion and stir-fry for another 2 minutes, or until the beef is cooked to your liking. Add the remaining marinade to the pan for the final minute.

Transfer to a plate to let the beef rest for around 3 minutes. You can cover it with foil to keep it warm.

Divide the noodle soup mixture between the bowls, then add the lovely beef. Drizzle over any remaining sauce, garnish with fresh chilli and coriander (cilantro if you like) and dive in.

- Serves 2
- Showing Off / One-Wok Wonder
- Wok to wonderful in 30 minutes
- Hero ingredient: mussels (page 22)

Stir-fried Mussels with Rice Noodles in Black Bean Sauce

Sea-saving-tummy-pleasing-loveliness

If salty sea flavours spiked with umami are your thing, this is noodle heaven. Iron-rich mussels are packed with nutrients and super-tasty, plus, they're really sustainable. You can replace the mussels with vegetables or chicken, if you like.

1½ tablespoons vegetable oil

400g (14-oz) fresh ho fun rice noodles, or you can use dried wide flat rice noodles, but these will need to be soaked or cooked first

1 teaspoon garlic paste, or 2 garlic cloves, crushed and finely chopped

1 tablespoon fermented salted soft black beans, rinsed in cold water

½ aubergine (eggplant), about 100g (3½oz), cut into 2.5–5cm (1–2in) fingers

½ green bell pepper, finely diced

½ red bell pepper, finely diced

1 small red onion, finely diced

220g (8oz) cooked mussels, meat only (no shell), fresh, frozen or tinned, (or use diced chicken breast)

FOR THE SAUCE:

½ tablespoon sake

1 teaspoon Mr Lee's Healthy Mussel Sauce (page 24), or ready-made fish sauce – increase to 2 teaspoons if using chicken

½ tablespoon toasted sesame oil

½ tablespoon crushed yellow bean sauce

½ tablespoon light soy sauce

½ tablespoon dark soy sauce

300ml (½ pint) boiling water or ready-made fresh fish or vegetable stock

1 tablespoon cornflour (corn starch) mixed with 1 tablespoon cold water

Place a wok over a high heat and add 1 tablespoon of the vegetable oil. Separate the noodles by hand, then add them to the wok. Fry the noodles for 3 minutes, then set aside on a large plate or bowl.

Return the wok to the heat and add the remaining ½ tablespoon oil. Add the garlic and black beans and stir for 30 seconds. Add the aubergine (eggplant), peppers and onions, followed by the mussels (or chicken), then pour the sake over the mixture and stir for just a few seconds. Next add the remaining sauce ingredients, except for the cornflour (corn starch) and water mixture. Stir and simmer for 2 minutes.

Finally add the cornflour and water mixture to the wok and stir as it thickens the sauce. Simmer for another 20–30 seconds. Pour the finished sauce over the warm noodles and serve immediately.

- Serves 2 as a main course, or 5–6 as a sharing dish
- Doddle / <15 Min / One-Wok Wonder
- Wok to wonderful in 15 minutes
- Hero ingredients: sesame oil and mushrooms (page 20/22)

Yi Mein Noodles with Fresh Crab (E-Fu)

Ain't No Party Like a Noodle Party

Traditionally served at parties in China, this tasty dish is known as 'Celebration Noodles'. The legend goes that a wealthy family asked their chef to make a delicious noodle dish that their guests could take home with them. Now you can enjoy this steaming bowl of noodle-y history. You'll find e-fu/yi mein noodles in Chinese supermarkets, or you can substitute with dried ramen noodles.

120g (4¼oz) fresh e-fu noodles, or use dried e-fu or ramen noodles

140ml (4¾fl oz) water or ready-made fresh vegetable stock

100g (3½oz) tinned straw mushrooms, well drained, or any tinned mushrooms

¼ tablespoon crushed yellow bean sauce

1 tablespoon Mr Lee's Healthy Mussel Sauce (page 24) or ready-made fish sauce

¼ teaspoon white pepper

few drops of toasted sesame oil

90–120g (3–4¼oz) cooked white crab meat, or cooked king prawns (jumbo shrimp), roughly chopped

sea salt (optional)

TO SERVE:

30g (1oz) brown crab meat, or ½ small carrot, finely diced (optional)

Mr Lee's Red Chilli Oil (page 29), to serve (optional)

Place the noodles in a large bowl and cover with boiling water for 1 minute, then drain immediately: this removes the excess oil from the fresh noodles. If using dried noodles, place a small saucepan of boiling water over a high heat, and simmer the noodles for 2½ until almost soft, then drain in colander and set aside.

Place a wok over a high heat and add the water or stock. Bring to the boil, then add the mushrooms, along with the yellow bean sauce, mussel fish sauce, white pepper and sesame oil. Mix well and cook for 30 seconds.

Then add that lovely sweet white crab meat (or prawns/ shrimp, if using), along with the noodles. Keep stirring until the sauce has reduced and the noodles have absorbed all the liquid and flavours. Season to taste, adding salt or a little more fish sauce if you like.

Sprinkle over some fresh brown crab meat or diced carrot, if you like. Serve immediately for 2 people as a main course, but these are really party noodles! So get some friends round to share, with some red chilli oil on the side.

 See picture overleaf (top left)

- Serves 2
- A Little Effort / Vegan Option
- Wok to wonderful in 15 minutes
- Hero ingredient: shiitake mushrooms (page 22)

Pork with Crispy Noodles & Yellow Bean Sauce

Good Times Noodles

In South China, Yum Cha is an afternoon tea tradition. You'd usually have it with friends over some dim sum. But it's so delicious, we think you should be able to enjoy it yourself! This combo of tangy, lip-smacking sauce with crispy noodles shouldn't have to wait until you've got people over. For a vegan option, just use your favourite meat substitute.

120g (4¼oz) dried thin wheat noodles

220g (8oz) pork fillet, thinly sliced (or use vegan mock meat, for a vegan alternative)

1 tablespoon vegetable oil

½ teaspoon garlic paste, or 1 small garlic clove, crushed and chopped

2–3 small carrots, thinly sliced

85g (3oz) fresh shiitake or oyster mushrooms, thinly sliced

300g (10½oz) bean sprouts

FOR THE MARINADE:

1 tablespoon crushed yellow bean sauce, or red or brown miso paste

1 tablespoon Mr Lee's Healthy Mussel Sauce (page 24) or ready-made fish sauce (or use Mr Lee's Vegan 'Fish' Sauce, page 25, for a vegan alternative)

1 tablespoon light soy sauce

½ teaspoon toasted sesame oil

¼ teaspoon ground white pepper

FOR THE SAUCE:

4 tablespoons American cream soda soft drink, or 100 per cent pineapple juice

1 tablespoon light soy sauce

½ tablespoon sake

300ml (½ pint) boiling water, or ready-made fresh vegetable or chicken stock

1 tablespoon cornflour (corn starch), made into a paste with 1 tablespoon cold water

Soak the noodles in a bowl of boiling hot water for 2–3 minutes, then drain and rinse in cold water. Drain again and set aside.

In a medium bowl, mix together the marinade ingredients. Add the pork or mock meat, stirring it up nicely. Set aside for a few minutes.

Place a wok over a high heat and add the vegetable oil. Add the noodles and toast them until they're nice and crispy. Transfer to a serving dish and use kitchen scissors to cut the noodles into bite-sized pieces.

Return the wok to the hob, and increase the heat to smoking-hot. Add the marinated pork or mock meat and fry for a few minutes, keeping any leftover marinade in the bowl. Then add the garlic, carrots, mushrooms and bean sprouts and stir-fry together for 1 minute.

Now add all of the sauce ingredients except the cornflour (corn starch) and water mixture. Stir well and cook over a high heat for 30 seconds. Keep stirring until the sauce thickens. If it needs a little help to thicken, add about half of the cornflour and water mixture and stir it in – this should thicken it up a bit. Add the remainder if needed, then cook for another 30 seconds. Stir the mixture well, then pour it on top of the noodles, along with any remaining marinade, and eat immediately.

See picture overleaf (top right)

- Serves 1
- Doddle / <15 Min / One-Wok Wonder / Gluten-Free / Vegan
- Wok to wonderful in 10 minutes
- Hero ingredient: chilli (page 20)

Warm Noodle Salad with Peanut Butter

Your Nutty Snack Lifesaver

When you want something quick and satisfying with a real flavour hit, forget crisps or PB&J: this is your healthy nutty hero. We're talking layer upon layer of flavour with a chilli spike that makes the whole thing super moreish. Perfect for a light snack or as a side dish, it also works really well with Cheung Fun rice noodle rolls (page 101).

60–85g (2–3oz) dried flat wide wheat noodles

FOR THE DRESSING:
¼ red onion, finely chopped
1 tablespoon peanut butter
1 tablespoon soy sauce
1 teaspoon finely chopped fresh red chilli
½ spring onion (scallion), finely chopped
1 tablespoon toasted sesame oil, peanut oil or vegetable oil

This is an absolute doddle. Mix together all the ingredients for the dressing in a small bowl and set it aside.

Half-fill a medium saucepan with boiling water and place over a high heat. Bring it back up the boil, and add the noodles. Simmer for 3 minutes, then drain. Put the noodles on a plate and top with the dressing. Either eat it warm or stick it in the fridge, ready for when the munchies strike.

See picture on previous page (bottom centre)

- Serves 2
- Doddle / <15 Min / One-Wok Wonder / Gluten-Free Option / Vegan
- Wok to wonderful in 15 minutes
- Hero ingredient: sesame seeds (page 20)

Ho Fun Macau

Forget Pret – Ho Fun's Where it's At

You'll typically find these thick, flat, chewy noodles everywhere from Hong Kong to Penang. Come 4pm, you can spot the locals' favourite ho fun restaurant by the size of the queue and the noisy racket of diners inside. Traditionally made with beef, you can use turkey, chicken, tofu or lots of lovely veg. In the West, we often pile it high with scallops, prawns, squid and mussels.

400g (14oz) fresh ho fun rice noodles, or 100g (3½oz) dried Thai-style flat rice noodles, 1cm (½in) wide
1 tablespoon vegetable oil
½ teaspoon garlic paste, or 1 garlic clove, crushed and chopped
1 small spring onion (scallion), finely sliced, white and green parts separated
1 tablespoon dark soy sauce (or tamari for a gluten-free alternative)
1 tablespoon light soy sauce (or tamari for a gluten-free alternative)
few drops of toasted sesame oil
¼ teaspoon sea salt, to taste
¼ teaspoon ground white pepper
200g (7oz) bean sprouts
1 tablespoon toasted sesame seeds

Using your hands, separate the rice noodles, then put them on a plate and microwave for 3 minutes. If you're using dried noodles, soak them in freshly boiled water for 10–15 minutes until softened, then drain well.

Heat the vegetable oil in a wok over a blisteringly high heat. Add the garlic and the white parts of the spring onion (scallion), along with the warm rice noodles. Stir-fry for 30 seconds, mixing it all up nicely.

Then add the light and dark soy sauce (or tamari), followed by the sesame oil, salt, white pepper and bean sprouts and keep stirring gently.

Pile the noodles on to a plate and sprinkle with the toasted sesame seeds. Scatter over the green parts of the spring onion and serve.

- Makes 12–14 wontons
- Showing Off / Vegetarian Option
- Wok to wonderful in 30 minutes
- Hero ingredient: ginger (page 22)

Turkey-stuffed Wonton Noodle Pastry with Red Oil Dressing

Not your Chrimbo Stodge-fest

A world away from your mum's (admittedly brilliant) Christmas dinner. This celebration dish from Hong Kong gives the festive bird an exotic twist. Get some friends round and give them these noodle-wrapped dumplings, which locals call sai yun – meaning small and silky.

plain flour, for dusting
1 egg yolk
12–14 wonton noodle/pastry wrappers
Mr Lee's Red Chilli Oil (page 29),
    to serve

FOR THE FILLING:
115g (4oz) minced (ground) turkey (or use
    vegan mince or firm tofu, finely chopped,
    for a vegetarian alternative)
½ spring onion (scallion), finely sliced
1 teaspoon ginger paste, or 2.5cm (1in)
    piece of fresh root ginger, finely chopped
1 tablespoon light soy sauce
1 tablespoon Mr Lee's Healthy Mussel Sauce
    (page 24), or ready-made fish sauce (or use
    light soy sauce or Mr Lee's Vegan 'Fish' Sauce,
    page 25, for a vegetarian alternative)

In a bowl, mix together all the filling ingredients. Use your hands to really squish it all together.

Prepare your work surface by dusting it with flour. Lightly whisk the egg yolk in a small cup. Separate the sheets of wonton pastry on to the floured surface and cover with a damp cloth or a plastic bag.

Lay a sheet of pastry in the palm of your hand and place a teaspoon of the filling mixture in the centre. Brush the whisked egg yolk on to one corner of the pastry, then fold the pastry from the opposite corner to form a triangle, squeezing lightly to seal. Put a bit more egg on to the two newly formed corners and fold these corners together, squeezing them together with your finger and thumb, under the chin of the dumpling and forming a tortellini-like shape. You've made your first wonton! First, allow yourself a little victory lap around the kitchen, then back to work. These wontons aren't going to make themselves.

Place the filled wonton on the floured surface, and repeat with the next wonton wrapper. Keep going until you've used up all the filling. If you want to freeze your wontons, lay them on a floured tray or in a wide container, then cover and place in the freezer. Once they've frozen, they can be bagged together.

To cook the wontons, half-fill a large saucepan with boiling water and place it over a high heat. Bring it to a rolling boil, then carefully put in your wontons into the water and let them bobble about for around 4 minutes. Gently lift the wontons from the water using a slotted spoon and lay in a large bowl or plate. Drizzle with red oil chilli and serve immediately.

- Serves 1 as light meal, or 2 as side dish
- Doddle / <15 Min / One-Wok Wonder / Vegan
- Wok to wonderful in 14 minutes
- Hero ingredients: sesame oil and spinach (page 20/21)

Sesame Spinach Lo Mein

Lean, Green Flavour Machine

Your mum's been trying to get you to eat your greens for years. Well, if this big-flavoured beauty doesn't convince you, nothing will. It brings out the best in Popeye's go-to green, spinach, and makes a great light meal or side dish. You can also use spinach pasta, or add fresh spinach to any dried wheat noodles to give them a hit of goodness.

55g (2oz) dried spinach noodles or dried spinach spaghetti (or use regular dried wheat noodles)
2 large handfuls fresh baby spinach leaves (optional)
½ tablespoon chopped spring onion (scallion)

FOR THE SAUCE:
½ tablespoon light soy sauce
½ tablespoon toasted sesame oil
½ tablespoon Japanese sesame sauce, or tahini paste

Mix together all the sauce ingredients in a bowl and set aside.

Half-fill a medium pan with boiling water. Place over a high heat and add the noodles (or pasta if you're using). Simmer for 2 minutes (or 8–10 minutes for dried pasta), then drain.

Return the drained noodles to the empty saucepan and add the dressing, along with the fresh spinach, if using. Mix it up so that everything's covered in that lovely sauce and the spinach gently wilts. Tip the noodles on to a large plate or bowl, sprinkle over the spring onion (scallion) and serve immediately.

- Serves 1 as a main (or 2 as side dish)
- Doddle / <15 Min / One-Wok Wonder / Vegetarian Option
- Wok to wonderful 15 minutes
- Hero ingredient: ginger (page 22)

Hong Kong-Style Lo Mein with Ginger & Spring Onion

Silky Smooth and Easy

This classic is a staple of every Chinese household because it goes with anything. It's great with our Healthy Mussel Sauce (page 24) and works with your favourite proteins, such as grilled chicken, fish or tofu. Or if you want to go veggie, use mushroom stir-fry sauce (or Mr Lee's Vegan 'Fish' Sauce, page 25). You can substitute any yellow dried egg noodle, or even a vegan yellow noodle.

few drops of toasted sesame oil
2.5cm (1in) piece of fresh root ginger, sliced into thin strips, or use 1 tablespoon ginger paste
½ spring onion (scallion), finely sliced
½ tablespoon dark soy sauce
½ tablespoon Mr Lee's Healthy Mussel Sauce (page 24), or use mushroom stir-fry sauce for a vegetarian alternative
85g (3oz) dried lo mein or yellow noodles

Place a wok over a high heat and add a few drops of sesame oil. After 20 seconds, add the ginger and spring onion (scallion) and stir-fry for another 10 seconds. Remove from the heat, add the soy sauce and mussel (or mushroom) sauce and set aside .

Half-full a medium saucepan with boiling water. Add the noodles and cook for 2 minutes, then drain in a colander or sieve, giving it a little shake to remove any excess water. Tip the noodles into the wok and mix well to coat in the sauce ingredients. Serve immediately on a large plate.

- Serves 2
- Doddle / <15 Min / Gluten-Free / Vegan Option
- Wok to wonderful in 14 minutes
- Hero ingredient: garlic (page 20)

Cheung Fun: Rice Roll Noodle Stir-fry

Rice and Roll Star!

You might have to hunt these rice rolls down at your local Chinese supermarket or online, but they're worth it. They bring new textures that will take your noodle game to the next level. Cheung refers to the sausage-like shape of the noodle. Try them with Mr Lee's Hoisin Sauce (page 25) or the spicy peanut butter dressing from the Warm Noodle Salad on page 90.

½ tablespoon vegetable oil

½ tablespoon garlic paste, or 1 garlic clove, crushed and chopped

¼ spring onion (scallion), finely sliced

400g (14oz) fresh cheung fun rice noodle rolls, each cut into 4–5 chunky pieces

200g (7oz) bean sprouts

1 tablespoon Mr Lee's Healthy Mussel Sauce (page 24), or ready-made fish sauce (or use Mr Lee's Vegan 'Fish' Sauce, page 25, for a vegan alternative)

pinch of ground white pepper

pinch of sea salt, to taste

5– 6 Thai basil leaves, or use Italian or Greek basil

TO GARNISH:

1 tablespoon peanuts, roughly chopped

¼–½ fresh red chilli, finely chopped, to taste

2 lime wedges

Heat the vegetable oil in a wok over a high heat. Add the garlic, spring onion (scallion) and cheung fun. Stir-fry for 3–4 minutes, keeping it all moving nicely.

Add the beansprouts, fish sauce (or vegan alternative), salt, white pepper and basil, mixing everything together well and cooking for another minute.

Transfer the noodle mixture to a serving dish and sprinkle with the peanuts and chilli. Finish with a squeeze of lime juice and serve.

- Serves 2 (makes 12–14 wontons)
- Showing Off
- Wok to wonderful in... well, that depends. How fast can you make wantons? 30 minutes with practice.
- Hero ingredient: ginger (page 22)

Cantonese-style Wonton Soup

Rule-breaking Bad Boy

Yeah, we know we said all of the recipes take 30 minutes or less. But this wonton noodle soup doesn't care about the human construct you call time. Once you taste it, you won't either. There is nothing more soul-warming than a steaming bowl of wonton soup. We've given it a Mr Lee's twist by using some healthier alternatives in the filling and taken some clever shortcuts.

300g (10½oz) large raw prawns (shrimp), shell on
few drops toasted sesame oil
1 tablespoon mirin
100g (3½oz) minced (ground) turkey
2 rashers turkey bacon, finely chopped
¼ teaspoon sea salt, to taste
small pinch of ground white pepper
flour, for dusting
1 egg yolk
12–14 wonton noodle/pastry wrappers
200g (7oz) pak choi (bok choy), leaves separated, and torn if large
Mr Lee's Red Chilli Oil, to serve (page 29)

FOR THE BROTH:
½ tablespoon vegetable oil
1 teaspoon ginger paste, or 2.5cm (1in) piece of fresh root ginger, finely chopped
115g (4oz) minced (ground) pork
900ml (1½ pints) boiling water
½ –1 teaspoon sea salt, to taste
¼ teaspoon ground white pepper

First peel the prawns (shrimp). You should end up with about 120g (4¼oz) shelled prawn meat. Keep the shells to use in the broth.

To make the broth, place a medium saucepan over a very high heat and add the vegetable oil. When smoking hot, add the prawn shells and ginger and fry for 4 minutes, browning the shells. Next add the minced (ground) pork, and fry for a further 2 minutes. Now pour in the boiling water and bring to the boil, then simmer for 20 minutes. Add the salt and

pepper, and adjust the seasoning to taste if needed.

While the broth is simmering, prepare the wonton filling. Remove the dark veins of the prawns by slicing them down the back, from tail to head, then dice the prawn meat. Place the diced meat in a bowl and mix in the sesame oil, mirin, minced (ground) turkey and turkey bacon. Season with salt and pepper. Use your hands to ensure the ingredients are well blended together. You can get messy or wear food-safe gloves if you prefer.

To make the wontons, prepare your work surface by dusting it with flour. Lightly whisk the egg yolk in a small cup. Separate the sheets of wonton pastry on to floured surface and cover with a damp cloth or a plastic bag.

Lay a sheet of pastry in the palm of your hand and place a teaspoon of the filling mixture in the centre. Brush the whisked egg yolk on to one corner of the pastry, then fold the pastry from the opposite corner to form a triangle, squeezing lightly to seal. Put a bit more egg on to the two newly formed corners and fold these corners together, squeezing them together with your finger and thumb, forming a tortellini-like shape.

Place the filled wonton on the floured surface, and repeat with the next wonton wrapper. Keep going until you've used up all the filling. If you want to freeze your wontons, lay them on a floured tray or in a wide container, then cover and place in the freezer. Once they've frozen, they can be bagged together.

To cook the wontons, half-fill a large saucepan with boiling water and place it over a high heat. Once the water reaches a good rolling boil, gently add the wontons to the water. Reduce the heat slightly to

medium–high
and simmer
the wontons
for 2–3 minutes.
Add the pak
choi (bok choy)
to the water and
cook for another
10–20 seconds.
Using a slotted spoon,
lift the wontons and
vegetables from the water
and lay into two large, deep
soup bowls.

Using a fine sieve, pour the
broth over the wontons, dividing
the soup equally between the bowls.
Serve immediately.

Although heavily influenced by its Chinese cousin, Japanese cuisine is completely its own thing. First, let's talk about seafood. Japan consists of nearly 7,000 islands, so as you can imagine, the seafood is incredible. And they know how to get the best out of it.

In terms of flavour, there's a real subtlety to Japanese food. It seduces you with delicately balanced flavours so that before you know it, you're completely in love. This ability to balance different textures and sweetness with saltiness is a signature of Japanese cooking.

In this section, you'll find the Japanese classics loved in every home from Wakkanai to Kagoshima, along with some gorgeous ramens and some discoveries from our own travels.

In true Mr Lee's style, we're going to make it all tasty, fast and healthy. We'll show you how to skip the 24-hour broth making, but still pack in the flavour. You'll learn how to combine Japanese flavours like miso, mirin, sake and tamari to give you deep and flavourful sauces.

We'll focus on the noodle that took over the world, ramen, but we'll also introduce you to some challengers to the title, like udon and the super-healthy buckwheat (soba) noodle. All without any nasties, and pimped up with nutrient-rich proteins.

In Japan, they don't just say delicious – they say 'Hoppe ga ochiru', which translates as 'So delicious my cheeks will fall off'. So that's our aim. To make your cheeks fall off.

3

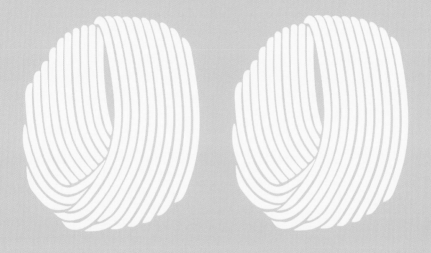

Japanese

Teriyaki Chicken Ramen Soup

Everybody loves Ramen

The undisputed king of comfort foods. This chicken ramen is the soupy equivalent of a reassuring cuddle from someone you adore. In true Mr Lee's style, we've made it simple and easy to get your comfort on. The broth is boosted by the flavourful mince and miso to give it a deep umami richness.

2 teaspoons vegetable oil
240g/14oz chicken breasts or boneless thighs
   (or use firm tofu for a vegetarian alternative)
110ml (4fl oz) Mr Lee's Healthy Teriyaki Sauce (page 25)
940ml (1¾ pints) ready-made fresh chicken or good
   quality vegetable stock, or use boiling water
2 tablespoons sweetcorn kernels
2 teaspoons white miso paste, or brown/red miso paste
400g (14oz) fresh ramen noodles
1 teaspoon rice vinegar, or any kind of vinegar
2 eggs

TO SERVE:
¼ iceberg lettuce, finely sliced
2 teaspoons salted butter
2 spring onions (scallions), finely chopped

Heat the oil in a medium-sized saucepan over a medium heat. Add the chicken and pan-fry for 1 minute on each side.

Add the teriyaki sauce and cook the chicken for a further 4 minutes over a high heat one side. Flip the chicken, and cook for another 4 minutes, reducing the teriyaki sauce. Remove the chicken from the pan and set aside.

Add the stock (or boiling water, if using) to the remaining teriyaki sauce left in the saucepan. Stir in the sweetcorn and miso paste, bring to boil and simmer for 2 minutes.

Meanwhile, half-fill another saucepan with boiling water and place over a high heat. Add the noodles and boil for 2 minutes. Lift the noodles from the pan of hot water using a slotted spoon and divide them between two large, deep serving bowls. Add the vinegar to the saucepan of water, bring back to the boil and carefully crack the eggs into the water. Poach for 2 minutes for a soft yolk.

While your eggs are poaching, pour the soup broth over the noodles, placing the sweetcorn to one side and pouring the last of the broth on top of the noodles in each bowl. Place the iceberg lettuce next to the sweetcorn at the side of each bowls.

Slice the chicken, lay it on top of the lettuce and place a small knob of butter on top of the sweetcorn. Now, using a slotted spoon, carefully lift the poached eggs from the boiling water, gently shaking off the excess water, and lay on the top of the bowl like a little eggy crown. Slice the eggs in half using a sharp knife. Sprinkle the spring onion (scallion) over the top of each bowl and serve immediately.

- Serves 2
- Doddle / <15 Min / One-Wok Wonder / Vegan
- Wok to wonderful in 10 minutes
- Hero ingredients: seaweed and edamame beans (page 20/23)

Creamy 'Butter' Udon Noodles with Seaweed

Buttering up the Vegans

Love creamy, buttery flavours and vegan food? This one's for you. Udon are the thickest of all Japanese noodles and come from the south. In this dish, the nutrient-packed seaweed gives you lots of plant-protein goodness. The Japanese add the aromatic togarashi after a few mouthfuls so they can vary the flavours of the dish. Give it a go – you'll love it.

400g (14oz) fresh udon noodles, or use fresh pasta, such as extra-thick spaghetti, but this is unlikely to be vegan so check label
2 heaped tablespoons frozen edamame beans (soybeans)
½ teaspoon dried seaweed, such as dulse or wakame
1 tablespoon vegetable oil
2 tablespoons finely chopped spring onion (scallion)
½ nori sheet, cut into triangles or squares (optional)
pinch of togarashi (shichimi or Japanese seven-spice), to serve

FOR THE SAUCE:
120ml (4fl oz) unsweetened soy milk
2 tablespoons mirin
2 tablespoons sake
1 tablespoon tamari
½ teaspoon sea salt, to taste
½ teaspoon ground white pepper

Half-fill a medium saucepan with boiling water and place over a high heat. Add the udon noodles, edamame beans and dried seaweed to the hot water for 10 seconds, then drain and set aside.

Heat the oil in a wok over a high heat. Add the drained noodles and seaweed, along with all the sauce ingredients. Mix well and stir for 45 seconds. Divide the noodles between 2 bowls and top with the chopped spring onion (scallion) and nori pieces, if using. Serve immediately, with togarashi on the side.

- Serves 2
- Doddle / <15 Min / One-Wok Wonder
- Wok to wonderful in 15 minutes
- Hero ingredient: sesame seeds (page 20)

JAPANESE

Sesame Prawns with Udon Noodles

Protein-packed Perfection

This quick and easy dish makes the most of sweet, protein-y prawns, pairing them perfectly with the bouncy udon noodles. In Japan, this is typically served as a soup, but we've tweaked it into a stir-fry and added some crunchy sweet leeks. Japanese sesame sauce is available in most supermarkets. But you can always use tahini paste as a substitute.

400g (14oz) fresh udon noodles, or use fresh pasta, such as extra-thick spaghetti
½ tablespoon vegetable oil
250g (9oz) fresh or frozen peeled king prawns (jumbo shrimp), defrosted if frozen
½ leek, finely sliced at an angle
½ teaspoon toasted black sesame seeds, to garnish (optional)

FOR THE STIR-FRY SAUCE:
1½ tablespoons tamari
1 tablespoon mirin
1 tablespoon sake
1 tablespoon Japanese sesame sauce or tahini paste

Place the fresh udon noodles in a large bowl and cover with boiling water. Soak for 10 seconds, then drain and set aside. If using fresh pasta, cook according to packet instructions and set aside.

Heat the oil in a wok over a very high heat. Add the prawns (shrimp) to the very hot wok (note to self: Hot Wok would make an awesome title for Mr Lee's first album) and allow them to colour for 20 seconds. Turn and fry for another 20 seconds on the other side, then remove from the wok and set aside on a plate.

Return the wok to the high heat and add the leek. Stir-fry for 20 seconds, then add the drained noodles, along with the stir-fry sauce ingredients. Really mix it up well so all those flavours can get to know each other. Now return the prawns (shrimp) to the wok and continue to stir-fry for another 2 minutes.

Pile all the noodles on to a large serving platter, scatter with sesame seeds if using, and serve immediately.

- Serves 2
- Doddle / <15 Min / One-Wok Wonder
- Wok to wonderful in 15 minutes
- Hero ingredient: bell pepper (page 23)

Curry Chicken Stir-Fry Ramen

Curry AND Ramen? Might as well end the book here

Bring together the punchy spiciness of your favourite curry with the fresh comfort of a ramen. For us, chicken thighs are more flavourful than breast, but go with what you like. You can also substitute chicken for vegan mock chicken or some fresh, tender veggies. You'll usually find fresh ramen noodles vac-packed on the shelf or in the fridge at your local supermarket.

250g (9oz) chicken thighs or breast, chopped into bite-sized pieces
350g (12oz) fresh ramen noodles, or 120g (4¼oz) dried wheat or egg noodles
½ tablespoon vegetable oil
½ onion, finely sliced
100g (3½oz) white cabbage, finely sliced
1 small carrot, cut into thin strips
½ red bell pepper finely sliced
½ teaspoon salt, or to taste
¼ teaspoon ground white pepper, or to taste
1 tablespoon shredded red cabbage or red onion (optional) to serve

FOR THE MARINADE:
½ tablespoon tamari
1 tablespoon medium curry powder
½ teaspoon garam masala
¼ teaspoon chilli powder

FOR THE STIR-FRY SAUCE:
1½ tablespoons tamari
1 tablespoon mirin
½ tablespoon medium curry powder
1–2 tablespoons water

First things first, prepare the marinade. Mix together all the marinade ingredients in a medium bowl. Add the chicken and mix so that it's all nicely coated. Set aside for 5 minutes.

Place the fresh noodles in a large bowl and pour over enough boiling water to cover. Soak for 10 seconds, then drain and set aside. If you're using dried noodles, place them in a saucepan of boiling water and simmer over a medium heat for 5–6 minutes, depending on how chewy you like your noodles. Drain and set aside.

Place a wok over a very high heat and add the vegetable oil. Then add the marinated chicken pieces, along with any marinade in the bowl, and stir-fry for 3 minutes. Add the onion, white cabbage, carrot and bell pepper and season with the salt and pepper. Now add the drained noodles and all of the sauce ingredients. Mix really well to make sure everything is combined. Continue to stir-fry for another 2–3 minutes.

Pile all the noodles on to a large serving platter, top with the shredded crunchy red cabbage or red onion (if using), grab your chopsticks and dive into a curry-ramen wonderland.

- Serves 2
- Showing Off / Vegan Option / Crowd-Pleaser
- Wok to wonderful in 30 minutes
- Hero ingredients: enoki mushrooms, ginger, miso, seaweed (page 20-23)

Tonkotsu Pork Ramen

24-hour Pork in 30 Minutes

Haven't got time to boil bones for 24 hours and slow-cook pork? Nah, us neither. Good thing we've come up with a short cut to give you a deeply flavoured stock in less than 30 minutes. If you don't want to use pork, you can use tofu instead. This is often served with togarashi. Start by enjoying the broth as it is, then use the spice mix to transform the flavour halfway through.

220g (8oz) pork fillet (or use firm tofu for a vegan alternative), sliced into 0.5cm (¼in) slices

2 tablespoons tamari

¾ tablespoon honey (or use agave syrup for a vegan alternative)

360g (12¾oz) fresh ramen noodles, or 100g (3½oz) dried wheat or egg noodles

½ tablespoon dried black fungus, shredded (optional)

75g (2¾oz) bean sprouts

50g (1¾oz) bamboo shoots, tinned or fresh, sliced, drained and rinsed

50g (1¾oz) fresh enoki mushrooms

½ nori sheet, cut into strips

2 soft-boiled eggs (leave these out for the vegan alternative)

1 spring onion (scallion), finely sliced

togarashi (shichimi or Japanese seven-spice), or just use chilli powder, to serve

FOR THE SOUP BASE:

300g (10½oz) minced (ground) pork (or use an additional 1 tablespoon of white miso paste for a vegan alternative)

1 tablespoon white miso paste

½ tablespoon smooth peanut butter

1 tablespoon sesame seeds

½ teaspoon ginger paste, or 2cm (¾in) piece of fresh root ginger, finely chopped

1 teaspoon garlic paste, or 2 garlic cloves, crushed and finely chopped

800ml (1½ pints) boiling water or ready-made fresh pork or vegetable stock

2 tablespoons sake

1 tablespoon mirin

2 tablespoons tamari

Place a medium saucepan over a high heat and add the minced (ground) pork for the soup base, if using. Brown for a minute or two, then add the remaining soup base ingredients. Mix well and reduce the heat slightly. Leave to simmer for 20 minutes.

Place the sliced pork or tofu in a bowl and pour over the tamari. Let it marinate for 5–10 minutes until the tamari has been absorbed.

Place a small frying pan (skillet) over a high heat and add the marinated pork or tofu pieces. Fry for 2 minutes on each side, then drizzle over the honey or agave. Continue to stir-fry for another minute, turning at least once, then remove from the heat and set aside.

Half-fill a medium saucepan with boiling water and place over a medium heat. Add the noodles and dried black fungus (if using) and bring to the boil. Reduce the heat and simmer for 3 minutes if you're using fresh noodles, or up to 10 minutes if you're using dried noodles.

Drain the noodles and divide them equally between 2 large soup bowls (although, in fairness, you did cook it – so maybe not that equally!). Add a small handful of bean sprouts to each bowl, then, using a sieve to strain it, pour the boiling hot broth into the bowls, and discard the solids in the sieve.

Top each bowl with slices of pork or tofu, bamboo shoots, enoki, nori strips and a boiled egg (if using). Sprinkle with the spring onion (scallion) and serve immediately, with togarashi on the side.

Serves 2

Doddle / <15 Min /
One-Wok Wonder /
Vegan Option

Wok to wonderful in
15 minutes

Hero ingredients: spinach
and salmon (page 20/21)

Fridge-raider Ramen with Smoked Salmon

The Works-with-everything Ramen

Pretty much goes with whatever you've got in your fridge. Leftovers from your Sunday roast, any veggies that have been hanging around – it can all can be transformed into noodle-y deliciousness. It works particularly well with smoked salmon, so that's what we're using here.

1 teaspoon vegetable oil

1 small carrot, peeled and cut into 5cm (2in) sticks

2 teaspoons dried garlic flakes, or 2 garlic cloves, thinly sliced

400g / 14oz fresh ramen noodles, or fresh egg noodles

2 teaspoons mirin

1 tablespoon tamari

2 teaspoons dark soy sauce

100g (3½oz) mangetout (snow peas)

2 handfuls of fresh baby spinach

175g (6oz) smoked salmon (or use smoked tofu, diced into 1cm (½in) pieces, or 4 large sun-dried tomatoes, finely chopped, for a vegan alternative)

2 spring onions (scallions), sliced, to garnish (optional)

Heat the vegetable oil in a wok over a high heat. Add the carrots and stir-fry for 45 seconds. Add the garlic and the noodles, mix well, and stir-fry for another 45 seconds.

Add the mirin, tamari and soy sauce to the pan, along with the mangetout (snow peas) and spinach. If you're using tofu or sun-dried tomatoes instead of salmon, add now. Mix everything well and stir-fry for another minute.

Pile the noodles on to a large serving platter, then tear the smoked salmon into pieces and sprinkle on top. Scatter over the spring onions (scallions), if using, and dive in.

THE NOODLE COOKBOOK

Honey-glazed Sea Bass with Ginger, Broccoli & Egg Noodles

Pump Up the Bass

Adored by fish lovers all over the world for its delicate flavour, sea bass is perfect for Japanese cooking. This recipe pumps up the bass with spikes of ginger, crunchy broccoli and crispy sweet and savoury skin. Minimum effort, maximum health and flavour. That's the Mr Lee's way.

2 x 125–140g (4-5oz) fresh sea bass fillets, skin on

2 teaspoons red miso paste

2 teaspoons honey

120g (4¼oz) dried egg noodles

150g (5½oz) sprouting broccoli, or use regular broccoli cut into bite-sized pieces

1 tablespoon vegetable oil, plus ½ teaspoon extra

4 tablespoons ginger paste, or 10cm (4in) fresh root ginger, finely chopped

2 tablespoons tamari

2 teaspoons toasted sesame oil

2 teaspoons rice vinegar

Using a sharp knife, lightly score the skin of the sea bass fillets with 3–4 slashes. In a small bowl, mix together the red miso and honey and rub the mixture on to the skin side of each fillet. Set aside on a plate for a few minutes at room temperature to let those flavours infuse into the fishies.

Meanwhile, half-fill a medium saucepan with boiling water and place over a high heat. Add the noodles and broccoli, and simmer for 4 minutes. Drain and set aside.

Heat 1 tablespoon of the oil in a wok over a high heat. When it's so smoking hot that you're starting to get worried about your smoke alarm, then it's hot enough. Lay the sea bass fillets gently into the pan, skin-side down. Cook for 3–4 minutes until the skin is crisp and golden brown. You can take a peek to see how they're getting on, but try not to fiddle with them too much.

Turn each fillet over and turn off the heat immediately. Let the fish stand in the hot pan for 2–3 minutes – again, don't mess about with it. Then, gently lift the fillets back on to a plate and set aside.

Return the same pan to a high heat and add the ½ teaspoon of oil, along with the ginger and the broccoli and noodles. Mix well on a high heat for 30 seconds, then add the tamari, sesame oil and rice vinegar. Stir-fry for another minute.

Pile the noodles on to a serving plate, and lay the fish, skin-side up, on top of the noodles. Serve immediately.

Miso-glazed Sesame Pork with Aubergine & Stir-fried Ramen

A Healthy Pig-out

This tasty little number uses lean pork fillet to give you a healthier piggy hit. The marinade is nutty and sweet in all the right places and pretty much goes with anything. Make a tub of this moreish marinade and stick it in the fridge for flavour emergencies. If you're not a pork lover, or want to try a vegan option, you can always make it using just aubergine (eggplant).

125g (4½oz) pork fillet, thickly sliced (or use 1 whole aubergine/eggplant thickly sliced lengthways for a vegan alternative, omitting the diced quantity below)

½ medium aubergine (eggplant), cut into 2.5cm (1in) dice

400g (14oz) fresh ramen noodles, or 120g (4½oz) dried wheat noodles

200g (7oz) bean sprouts

½ tablespoon vegetable oil

½ onion, finely sliced

1 teaspoon garlic paste, or 2 garlic cloves, crushed and finely chopped

2 tablespoons frozen edamame beans, roughly chopped

toasted sesame seeds, to serve

FOR THE MARINADE:

1 tablespoon tamari

1 teaspoon Japanese sesame sauce or use tahini paste

½ teaspoon ground white pepper

1 teaspoon red, brown or white miso paste

FOR THE STIR-FRY SAUCE:

2 tablespoons tamari

1 tablespoon dark soy sauce

1 tablespoon mirin

In a medium bowl, mix together all the marinade ingredients and add the pork and/or aubergine (eggplant) pieces. Mix it all up, then set aside for 5–10 minutes to let the flavours infuse and intensify.

Meanwhile, half-fill a medium-sized saucepan with boiling water. If you're using fresh noodles, add the noodles and bean sprouts and cook for 10 seconds, then drain immediately. If you're using dried noodles, add them to the pan and boil for 4–5 minutes (depending on how chewy you like them), then add the bean sprouts at the end for the final 10 seconds. Drain and set aside.

Heat the oil in a large wok over a high heat. Lay the pork and/or aubergine pieces carefully into the wok. Fry for 1 minute, then turn the pieces and fry for another minute on the other side. Add the onion, edamame and garlic, and stir-fry for another 30 seconds. Then add the noodles and bean sprouts, along with all the sauce ingredients. Mix everything together well and stir-fry for another 1½ minutes.

Pile the noodles on to a large plate, laying the pork and/or aubergine on top, then scatter with toasted sesame seeds and serve immediately.

- Serves 2
- Doddle / <15 Min / Vegan / Gluten-Free Option
- Wok to wonderful in 6 minutes
- Hero ingredients: buckwheat, seaweed, miso and spinach (page 20-21)

Buckwheat Noodles with Bamboo & Seaweed

Superfoods Don't Get Much…Erm…Super-er

Buckwheat, seaweed, miso, spinach…it's all soooo good for you. This recipe uses soba noodles, which is the Japanese name for buckwheat. Soba is a huge favourite across Japan and it contains all eight essential amino acids. The bamboo shoots give you some crunchy sweetness in this pimped-up miso broth, and you can add your favourite protein, like chicken, prawns or tofu.

100g (3½oz) dried soba (buckwheat) noodles
100g (3½oz) tinned sliced bamboo shoots, drained and rinsed

FOR THE SOUP:
850ml (1½ pints) boiling water
1 tablespoon white miso paste, or brown or red miso paste
1½ tablespoons sake
1½ tablespoons mirin
1 tablespoon dried wakame seaweed, or any seaweed you prefer

TO SERVE:
small handful of watercress or baby spinach
½ spring onion (scallion), finely chopped
few drops of toasted sesame oil

Place all the soup ingredients into a small saucepan over a high heat. Once it's simmering, add the noodles and bamboo shoots and cook for a further 2 minutes.

Place the watercress or spinach at the bottom of a deep serving bowl. Pour the noodle soup over the spinach.

Sprinkle the top with spring onion (scallion) and a few drops of toasted sesame oil. That's it – you're good to go!

Teriyaki Mushroom Medley with Rice Noodles

Meat-free, but Meaty. If That Makes Sense

This recipe uses an array of Japanese mushrooms to give you a hit of meaty plant-based goodness. If you can't find the mushrooms we've suggested, any supermarket selection pack of Asian/Japanese mushrooms works. The sweet, caramelised teriyaki goes beautifully with the earthy mushrooms, and the crunchy bean sprouts add a bonus layer of texture and flavour.

½ tablespoon vegetable oil

70g (2½oz) hen-of-the-woods (maitake) mushrooms, torn into large bite-sized strips (or use oyster mushrooms)

1 king oyster (eryngi) mushroom, thickly sliced lengthways (or use a large field mushroom)

70g (2½oz) shimeji or enoki mushrooms, torn into large bite-sized pieces

5 teaspoons Mr Lee's Healthy Teriyaki Sauce (page 25)

100g (3½oz) dried rice vermicelli noodles

100g (3½oz) bean sprouts, or use grated carrot and/or courgette

1 spring onion (scallion), green part only, finely sliced

FOR THE SAUCE:

600ml (20fl oz) boiling water

2 teaspoons miso paste

½ tablespoon tamari

1 teaspoon toasted sesame oil

Heat the vegetable oil in a wok over a high heat. When it's smoking hot, add all the mushrooms. Brown well, turning as needed, for 2 minutes, then remove the pan from the heat and add 2 teaspoons of the teriyaki sauce. Stir well to coat. Take the mushrooms out of the pan and set aside on a small plate.

Return the pan to the heat and add all the sauce ingredients, along with the rice noodles and bean sprouts (or carrot and/or courgette). Add another teaspoon of teriyaki sauce for luck and give it all a good stir.

Divide the noodles between two bowls, then top with the mushrooms. Make sure you mix them up, so you can each get a taste of all the different types of mushroom. Scatter over the spring onion (scallion) greens. Drizzle each bowl with another teaspoon of teriyaki sauce and serve immediately.

See picture overleaf (bottom left)

Hirata Buns with Lotus Root & Quick Veg Pickle

Buns Worth Fighting Over

These pillowy little beauties have pretty much taken over East Asia. Perfect for sharing, as long as there's enough to go around, they pack all the flavours. You can always substitute the rolls for a soft wheat roll if you like and use the same filling. You can find lotus root in any Chinese supermarket, but if you can't find it, you can use water chestnut or even courgette.

---

4 hirata or bao buns, fresh or frozen, or use a soft wheat roll/bap

FOR THE PICKLE:
¼ small carrot, cut into matchsticks
¼ cucumber, deseeded and cut into matchsticks
large pinch of sea salt
1 tablespoon rice vinegar
pinch of dried chilli flakes
large pinch of toasted sesame seeds

FOR THE FILLING:
¼ tablespoon of vegetable oil
1 small section of fresh lotus root, peeled and sliced into 0.5cm (¼in) slices (or use tinned water chestnut or courgette)
¼ teaspoon sea salt
¼ teaspoon ground white pepper
10g (¼oz) fresh udon noodles, roughly chopped
½ tablespoon sake
1 tablespoon Mr Lee's Healthy Teriyaki Sauce (page 25)

First, let's get into the pickle. Place the carrot sticks, cucumber sticks, salt, rice vinegar and chilli flakes in a medium bowl and mix well. Sprinkle over the sesame seeds and set aside for 15 minutes.

Meanwhile, place a steamer over a large saucepan of water over a high heat. Place the buns in the steamer and cook for 10 minutes if fresh, or for 15 minutes if frozen. Alternatively, you can give them a cheeky blast in the microwave for 30 seconds.

Place a large frying pan (skillet) over a high heat with the oil, and add the lotus root slices (or water chestnut or courgette). Cook for 20 seconds, then add the salt, pepper, noodles, sake and teriyaki sauce. Turn off the heat and mix everything together well. Set aside.

To assemble, divide the lotus root mixture between the buns and top with the pickled vegetables. Serve immediately – no time to be polite, these little beauties go fast.

See picture overleaf (top left)

- Serves 2
- Showing Off /
One-Wok Wonder /
Vegetarian Option
- Wok to wonderful in
30 minutes
- Hero ingredients: banana,
miso and sesame sauce
(page 20/21)

Mr Lee's Cracking Katsu

Get Your Crunch On

See picture on previous spread (top right).

Katsu gets its name from the incredibly moreish crispy breadcrumb coating called panko. Now, when this was traditionally served in Japanese pubs, it was made with pig's stomach or intestines. We love a bit of offal, but we're ditching that and going with turkey. You can use chicken, if you like, or go veggie and use firm tofu.

60g (2¼oz) panko (Japanese breadcrumbs)

1 egg

2 turkey steaks (approx. 250g/ 4 ½oz), or use 250g (9oz) firm tofu for a vegetarian alternative

½ teaspoon sea salt

pinch of ground black pepper

2 tablespoons vegetable oil

400g (14oz) fresh udon noodles, or use fresh pasta, such as extra-thick spaghetti

dried chilli flakes, or freshly sliced chilli, to garnish (optional)

FOR THE SAUCE:

1 teaspoon garlic paste, or 1 garlic clove crushed and finely chopped

½ red onion, diced

1 just-ripe banana (approx. 80g/3oz) peeled, or 1 tablespoon honey or agave syrup

½ tablespoon brown miso paste, or red or white miso

½ teaspoon Japanese sesame sauce (page 17)

½ tablespoon tamari

1 teaspoon mirin

1 heaped teaspoon medium or hot curry powder

1 heaped teaspoon garam masala

½ teaspoon paprika

¼ teaspoon mild chilli powder

480ml (17fl oz) boiling water

½ teaspoon sea salt

Prepare the katsu by placing the panko breadcrumbs on a small plate or in a wide bowl. Crack the egg into another wide bowl and lightly beat with a fork.

If using tofu, slice lengthways down the middle into thinner 'steaks'. Season the turkey or tofu with the salt and pepper. Use one hand to dip the first turkey or tofu steak into the egg, making sure it's coated. Use the other hand to dip it into the panko. Using just that hand, cover the steak well with crumbs. Then lift it out with your 'egg hand' and dip it into the egg again. Then, using your 'panko hand', dip the steak into the crumbs once again, so that it has an extra-thick crispy outer. Double dipped = mega crunchy! Lay the crumbed steak on to a plate ready to cook, and repeat with the second one. Your hands should be an eggy mess. Be proud, you've made a beautiful thing.

Heat the vegetable oil in a large, wide frying pan (skillet) over a high heat. Drop a few crumbs of panko into the oil and, when it just sizzles, gently lay the crumbed steaks into the oil and fry on each side for 3 minutes. Then transfer the steaks to a plate with paper towels to drain the excess oil.

To make the sauce, remove the excess oil from the frying pan, return it to the heat, and add the garlic and onion, stir-frying for 10 seconds. Add the banana and mush it up in the pan using a fork. Add all the remaining sauce ingredients and stir well, then add the noodles. Mix everything together and cook for 3 minutes, stirring continuously. The sauce will reduce and be absorbed by the noodles. After 3 minutes, turn off the heat and add another 120ml (4fl oz) water, just to loosen it and make it saucy.

To serve, lay the breaded meat on a chopping board and slice thickly. Place in a deep bowl on top of the noodles. Sprinkle with dried chilli flakes or freshly sliced chilli (if using) and serve.

Serves 1

Doddle / <15 Min /
One-Wok Wonder / Vegan
/ Gluten-Free Option

Wok to wonderful in
10 minutes

Hero ingredient: miso,
seaweed (page 21/20)

JAPANESE

Super Simple
Miso Ramen

Pure Magic in a Bowl

Deeply flavourful and laced with healthy bacteria and enzymes, miso so good for you it borders on magical. Japanese people have a hearty bowl of miso broth every day. You can adapt this recipe to add cooked veg, meat or tofu. Not all miso pastes are the same. White is mellow, brown is earthy, and red is the bold-tasting bad boy of the group. Try them all and see which one you like.

large pinch of dried wakame seaweed,
  or other dried seaweed
380ml (12¾fl oz) boiling water
½ tablespoon tamari
1 teaspoon mirin
½ teaspoon toasted sesame oil
200g (7oz) fresh ramen noodles (or rice noodles
  for a gluten-free alternative)
1 heaped teaspoon miso paste of your choice,
  mixed with 2 tablespoons cold water to make
  a runny paste
½ spring onion (scallion), finely sliced (optional)

Place the wakame in a small saucepan and cover with the boiling water. Then add the tamari, mirin, toasted sesame oil and noodles, and bring to a simmer, then remove from heat.

This step is important: let the broth cool for 3–4 minutes before you add the miso. If you add it too soon, you'll kill all that healthy bacteria. So, after 3–4 minutes of cooling, add the cold miso liquid to the broth and mix so that it's well dissolved. Serve immediately, topped with the spring onion (scallion), if using.

- Makes 2
- Showing Off / One-Wok Wonder / Vegetarian Option
- Wok to wonderful in 30 minutes
- Hero ingredient: seaweed (page 20)

Mr Lee's Bun-less Noodle Burger of Brilliance

Wait, what?

A burger recipe in a noodle book? That's just the kind of fusion-cooking, convention-defying rebels we are at Mr Lee's. Treat it like a normal burger: a bit of cheese, some crispy salad, a dash of mayo – all good. If you want your noodle buns crispy, give them some drying time, then let them get hot and crispy before turning when cooking.

115g (4oz) dried ramen noodles
2 egg yolks
2½ teaspoons vegetable oil

large metal cooker cutter ring, 10cm (4in) ring mould or empty tin with both ends removed, oiled

FOR THE BURGER PATTIES (OR USE 2 LARGE READY-MADE VEGETARIAN BURGERS, FOR A VEGETARIAN ALTERNATIVE):
225g (8oz) lean minced (ground) beef (such as wagyu)
1 teaspoon togarashi (shichimi or Japanese seven-spice)
¼ teaspoon sea salt
¼ teaspoon ground black pepper
1 teaspoon Mr Lee's Healthy Teriyaki Sauce (page 25)

TO SERVE:
2 slices of American-style burger cheese
1 nori sheet, cut into cheese-slice-sized squares
2 tablespoons mayonnaise
1 teaspoon wasabi powder, or ½ teaspoon wasabi paste
4 iceberg lettuce leaves, or a handful of salad of your choice
1 large tomato, thickly sliced
½ red onion, sliced into rings

Half-fill a medium saucepan with boiling water and place over a high heat. Add the noodles and bring to boil, then simmer for 3 minutes. Drain, then spread out the noodles on a baking sheet or clean work top, leaving to air dry for a few minutes.

Meanwhile, if you're making your own burgers, mix together all the burger patty ingredients in a bowl and shape into two patties. Set aside until needed.

Next, place a large frying pan (skillet) over a high heat. Lightly oil the cookie cutter, ring mould, or can and place on the hot pan. In a medium-sized bowl, mix the noodles with the beaten egg yolks, then divide into 4 equal portions. Place one portion into the mould in the pan, and push down firmly with a spoon to make a thick, even layer. Cook for a minute, until it firms up then carefully lift the mould. Repeat with the remaining noodles to create 4 noodle 'bun' halves. Fry for 3–4 minutes on each side until golden and crisp, then set aside for later.

Wipe out the pan, and add 1 teaspoon oil. Place the patties (or vegetarian burgers, if using) into the pan. Cook, without moving, for about 2 minutes, then carefully flip the burgers and top each one with a nori sheet, followed by a slice of cheese. Cook for another minute or two, according to your liking (1 minute more for medium–rare, 2 minutes more for medium). If your frying pan has a lid, cover for the final minute and the cheese will melt like you're a burger pro. (If you are using ready-made vegetarian burgers, adjust the timings above according to the packet instructions.)

Meanwhile, in a small bowl or cup, whisk together the mayonnaise and the wasabi powder or paste until fully blended.

To assemble the burgers together, place a ramen 'bun' on a plate and top with some wasabi mayonnaise and lettuce or salad leaves. Gently lay the burger on top, then top with tomato and onion slices, and close with another ramen 'bun'. Serve immediately.

Serves 2

Doddle / <15 Min /
One-Wok Wonder /
Gluten-Free Option

Wok to wonderful in
10 minutes

Hero ingredient: sesame
oil (page 20)

Sake-seared Scallops with Udon Noodles

Juicy, Bite-y Brilliance

This dish is all about the ingredients, but you still take the credit! The chewy noodles combine with the savoury crunch of the celery and balance beautifully with the scallops. It works with fresh or frozen scallops, but for the good stuff, choose some juicy-fresh, hand-dived fat ones. But any seafood works really. If you'd like a gluten-free noodle alternative, try ho-fun rice noodles.

10–12 scallops (approx. 240g/8½ oz) fresh or frozen, or substitute for other seafood
1 teaspoon sea salt
½ teaspoon ground black pepper
90ml (6 tablespoons) sake
2 teaspoons vegetable oil
1 celery stalk, stringy parts removed (see Tip on page 36), cut into 5cm (2in) sticks
400g (14oz) fresh udon noodles (or use fresh ho fun rice noodles for a gluten-free alternative)
3 tablespoons tamari
2 teaspoons mirin
2 teaspoons toasted sesame oil
celery leaves, to garnish

Season the scallops with the salt and black pepper. Place a flat frying pan (skillet) over a high heat. Once it's smoking hot, carefully add the scallops. Once you've added the last one, turn them over, starting with the first one. You want to give them about 20 seconds on each side. Now add the sake. Keep the pan nice and hot so that you burn off the alcohol and caramelise the scallops.

Next, add the celery and stir-fry everything for another minute, then add the noodles. Finally, add the tamari, mirin and sesame oil and stir-fry for another 2 minutes, mixing all the flavours up.

Divide the noodle mixture between 2 plates with some of the scallops on top. Decorate with a few sprigs of celery leaf and serve immediately.

- Serves 2
- A Little Effort / <15 Min / One-Wok Wonder / Vegan
- Wok to wonderful in 15 minutes
- Hero ingredient: miso (page 21)

Supersonic Udon Noodles with Vegetables

Your Humpday Hero

This faff-free stir-fry will save you from the clutches of a ready meal. It can be made with whatever tender veggies you have knocking about in your fridge. The red miso makes a gorgeous sauce and gives a deeply savoury flavour to your veg. And the bouncy udon noodles finish it off nicely.

400g (14oz) fresh udon noodles, or 120g (4¼oz) dried wheat noodles
½ tablespoon vegetable oil
200g (7oz) white cabbage, finely sliced
85g (3oz) baby corn, sliced lengthways
85g (3oz) fine green beans, sliced lengthways
85g (3oz) daikon (also known as mooli or Asian radish), or turnip, sliced into thin 5cm (2in) strips
1 carrot, cut into fine sticks
½ red bell pepper, finely sliced
1 teaspoon sea salt
½ teaspoon ground black pepper
pickled pink ginger or pickled daikon (mooli), to serve

FOR THE STIR-FRY SAUCE:
2 tablespoons tamari
2 tablespoons mirin
2 tablespoons sake
2 tablespoons Japanese sesame sauce, or tahini paste
2 teaspoons red miso paste

Place the noodles in a large bowl and pour over boiling water to cover. If you're using fresh udon noodles, soak for 10 seconds, then drain. If you're using dried noodles, soak for 5–6 minutes, then drain and set aside.

Heat the oil in a wok over a super-hot heat. Add the cabbage, baby corn, green beans, daikon (or turnip) carrot and red pepper. Season with the salt and bell pepper and stir-fry for 1 minute.

Add the drained noodles and all the sauce ingredients to the wok. Mix well and keep stir-frying for 3 minutes more.

Pile the noodle mixture on to a large serving platter, top with pickled ginger or daikon (mooli), serve immediately and enjoy!

Serves 2

A Little Effort /
<15 Minutes /
Gluten-Free Option

Wok to wonderful in
15 minutes

Hero ingredients:
sesame sauce/seeds and
edamame (page 20/23)

JAPANESE

Sesame-seared Tuna with Edamame & Rice Noodles

Big Kahuna of Healthy Tuna

The famously Japanese fish markets are a must visit. Lots of haggling and live tuna-cutting demos. You'll see some fish go for the price of a decent car. We're going to show you how to get a restaurant-quality nutty sear to your fish. Look for healthy and sustainable pole and line, troll or hand-line caught albacore tuna steaks.

2 x 120g (4½oz) tuna steaks, about 2.5cm (1in) thick
4 teaspoons Japanese sesame sauce, or tahini paste
½ teaspoon sea salt
½ teaspoon ground white pepper
½ tablespoon vegetable oil
100g (3½oz) dried thin rice noodles
2 tablespoons frozen edamame beans (soybeans)
1 teaspoon toasted black sesame seeds,
   to serve (optional)
dollop of wasabi, to serve

FOR THE SAUCE:
1 tablespoon tamari
2 teaspoons mirin
2 teaspoons Japanese sesame sauce, or tahini paste

Smother each of the tuna steaks in 2 teaspoons of sesame sauce. Rub it on both sides of the steaks and leave to stand for a few minutes. Season the steaks with the salt and white pepper.

Heat the vegetable oil in a large frying pan (skillet) over a high heat. When the pan is smoking hot, gently lay the tuna steaks into the pan. Sear on one side for 1 minute, then turn each steak, turn off the heat and leave the fish to cook for a further 40–60 seconds in the hot pan. Remove the steaks from the pan and set aside on a plate to rest.

Half-fill a medium saucepan with boiling water and place over a high heat. Add the noodles and edamame beans. Bring to the boil and simmer for 3 minutes, then drain well and transfer to a large bowl. Add the sauce ingredients to the bowl and mix it all up well.

Divide the noodles between two serving plates or dishes. Thickly slice each steak and place on top of the noodles. Sprinkle toasted black sesame seeds over the tuna (if using), place a dollop of wasabi on the side of each plate and serve immediately.

Thailand: the land of smiles! For some, Thailand is the ridiculously idyllic islands and powder-soft sandy beaches of the south; for others it's the steamy, bustling, neon metropolis of Bangkok, or the misty, unspoilt mountainous regions of the north. We've all discovered Thailand in our own way, whether it's through hazy memories of backpacking or dreams of the perfect holiday that we keep meaning to get around to booking. Maybe next year – definitely next year! But whether you've visited this amazing place or not, the food is world-famous.

Thai food is a genius alchemy that effortlessly balances sweet, spicy, salty and sour, creating its own umami. Each region has a unique style, but you can broadly define Thai food into four different types: phat (fried), sam (spicy salads), tom (boiled food and soups), and gaeng/kaeng (curries).

You can see the coconutty influence of Malaysia in the southern dishes and the spicy saltiness of the old silk road in the northern dishes – Chiang Mai curries (like the one on page 150) are a great example of this. We've spent a lot of time in Thailand, learning the tricks and discovering some hidden gems. These are our top Thai noodle dishes. Authentically, unmistakably Thai, with some added Mr Lee's magic to make them quick, easy and healthy.

4

Thai

- Serves 2
- A Little Effort / <15 Min / One-Wok Wonder / Vegan Option / Street-Food Fave
- Wok to wonderful in 15 minutes
- Hero ingredient: It's Pad Thai, the whole dish is a hero! Ok then, tofu (page 21)

Pad Thai
The Bangkok Banger

Pad Thai sums up everything that's amazing about Thailand. Its tempting aromas waft out of every Bangkok side street (pro tip: always follow your nose in Thailand). We've replaced the sugar with healthier agave syrup and you can get good tamarind pulp from most supermarkets, just make sure you get the right kind (see page 18). Great fish sauce and soy sauce will give you that lip-smacking-saltiness.

120g (4¼oz) dried flat rice noodles
3 teaspoons vegetable oil
2–3 eggs (omit for vegan alternative)
12–16 large, raw king prawns (jumbo shrimp) with shells removed, approx. 170g/6oz, fresh or frozen, tail on if possible (omit for vegan alternative)
170g (6oz) firm tofu, cut into 2cm (¾in) batons (double the quantity if omitting prawns)
2 spring onions (scallions), finely sliced
200g (7oz) bean sprouts
small handful of Chinese chives (garlic chives), roughly chopped

FOR THE SAUCE:
3–4 tablespoons agave syrup (or honey, if not vegan)
4 tablespoons tamarind light brown pulp or paste (light brown), or 2 teaspoons of dark concentrate
2 tablespoons Mr Lee's Healthy Mussel sauce (page 24) or ready-made fish sauce (or Mr Lee's Vegan 'Fish' Sauce, page 25, for a vegan alternative)
3–4 tablespoons soy sauce
2 tablespoons cold water
3–4 teaspoons rice vinegar

FOR SERVING:
2–3 lime wedges
½ teaspoon dried chilli flakes for sprinkling (optional)
1 large or 2 small fresh chillies, finely sliced in 2 tablespoons of rice vinegar
small handful of freshly chopped coriander (cilantro)

1–2 teaspoons agave or honey (optional, to taste)
small handful of roasted peanuts or cashews, roughly chopped

Fill a large bowl with boiling water and soak the noodles for 10–20 minutes, depending on your preference – soft or chewy. Drain and set aside.

Meanwhile, in a small bowl, mix together all the sauce ingredients. Keep tasting to check that there's a nice balance of sweet, salty and sour flavours. Trust your palate and adjust the flavours with a little more fish sauce, tamarind, vinegar or agave until it's bang on.

Heat 1 teaspoon of the oil in a large wok over a high heat. Add the eggs (if using). Use a spatula to scramble them in the pan and cook until just set. Tip the scrambled eggy loveliness on to a side plate and set aside.

Wipe the wok and add the remaining 2 teaspoons oil, then place it over a very high heat. When it's properly smoking hot, add the prawns (if using) and stir-fry for 1 minute so they start to caramelise; turn them if they get carried away. Then add the tofu pieces and cook for a further 20 seconds.

Next add the noodles and spring onions (scallions), along with three-quarters of the bean sprouts. Stir-fry over a very high heat for 30 seconds, then add the sauce. Keep stir-frying for another 1 minute 30 seconds, mixing well, then take the wok off the heat. Add the scrambled eggs, the rest of the bean sprouts and the chopped chives, combining it all with the noodle mixture. It should be fairly loose and the noodles slippery. Add a splash of water if it's a bit dry.

Divide the noodle mixture between 2 large bowls or plates, sprinkling a few more chopped chives on top if you like. Serve alongside lime wedges, and small bowls of pickled chillies (plus dried flakes if using), coriander (cilantro), agave or honey, and chopped nuts. Crack open a Chang or Singha beer for that authentic Bangkok experience!

- Serves 2 as light meal
- Doddle / <15 Min / One-Wok Wonder
- Wok to wonderful in 15 minutes
- Hero ingredient: squid or crayfish (page 22/23)

Chilli Squid Noodles

Winner Winner, Squid for Dinner

You'll find this dish close to the coast, or anywhere that prides itself on good seafood. If you can't get hold of holy basil or Thai basil (usually easy to find in Chinese supermarkets), you can use regular basil with a pinch of ground aniseed. This is a restaurant-quality, squidy winner that you can whip up in 15 minutes for your mid-week dinner. Bit of noodle poetry for you there.

½ tablespoon vegetable oil

1 teaspoon garlic paste, or 2 garlic cloves, crushed and finely chopped

1 large red chilli, finely chopped

220g (8oz) fresh or frozen squid, sliced into 0.5cm (¼in) rings, or use other seafood, like shrimp or crayfish

¼ teaspoon salt

¼ teaspoon ground white pepper

100g (3½oz) bean sprouts

400g (14oz) fresh egg noodles

125g (4½oz) small cherry tomatoes, halved

½ tablespoon Mr Lee's Healthy Mussel Sauce (page 24), or ready-made fish sauce

1 teaspoon light soy sauce

small handful of fresh Thai basil

juice of ½ lime

Heat the vegetable oil in a large frying pan (skillet) over a very high heat. When it's smoking hot, add the garlic, chilli, squid, salt and pepper. Cook for 10 seconds, then remove from the heat. Tip the squid mixture on to a plate and set aside.

Reheat the same frying pan and add the bean sprouts, noodles, tomatoes, fish sauce and light soy sauce. Stir-fry for 30 seconds, then add the basil. Return the cooked squid to the pan and cook for another 10 seconds.

Remove the pan from the heat and squeeze lime juice on top. Pile on to a large plate and you are done.

● Serves 2   ● A Little Effort / Vegan / Gluten-Free   ● Wok to wonderful in 25 minutes   ● Hero ingredients: turmeric, ginger and lemongrass (pages 21-22)

THAI

Yellow Curry Noodle Soup (Kaeng Kari Jay)

A Creamy Cuddle of a Curry

This is a beautifully comforting curry noodle soup – more of a warming cuddle than a kick. Found all over southern Thailand, it traditionally uses a slippery rice noodle like vermicelli, but mung bean thread noodles or any thin noodle will work fine. It also plays nicely with all veggies and seafood. The ingredients are easy to find, just blend it together and you're done.

½ tablespoon vegetable oil

85g (3oz) lotus root (fresh, jarred or frozen) peeled and sliced (see Tip), or cauliflower, cut into florets

450ml (16fl oz) vegetable stock or water, plus extra if needed

1 tablespoon Mr Lee's Vegan 'Fish' Sauce (page 25, made with tamari instead of soy)

½ tablespoon agave syrup (or honey, if not vegan)

85g (3oz) green beans, fresh or frozen

85g (3oz) mangetout (snow peas)

60g (2¼oz) Chinese broccoli (gai lan), roughly chopped, or fresh spinach, choi sum or pak choi (bok choy)

200ml (7fl oz) good-quality coconut milk

1 teaspoon sea salt, or to taste

1 tablespoon tamarind pulp (light brown type), or use ½ teaspoon of paste (dark brown)

120g (4½oz) dried thin rice noodles

FOR THE CURRY PASTE:

7.5cm (3in) piece of fresh root turmeric, or 1 teaspoon ground turmeric

¼ teaspoon paprika

2 teaspoons garlic paste, or 4 garlic cloves, peeled

5cm (2in) piece of fresh root ginger, peeled

4 whole dried red chillies, soaked in boiling water for 15 minutes (or use 1 teaspoon dried red chilli flakes)

½ small red onion, peeled and halved

1 fat lemongrass stalk, ends trimmed and outer layer removed, or 1 teaspoon ground dried lemongrass

4 kaffir lime leaves, fresh, frozen or dried

TO SERVE:

1 lime, halved

2 tablespoons roasted peanuts, roughly chopped (optional)

drizzle of red chilli oil (page 29), optional

Place all the curry paste ingredients in a blender or food processor and blitz until it forms a smooth paste. See, what did we say? Easy-peasy, limey squeezy!

Now heat the oil in a large wok over a medium–low heat and add the curry paste. If you're using fresh lotus root (or cauliflower), add it now, too. Gently fry for 2 minutes, then add the stock or water, vegan fish sauce or tamari, and agave. Increase the heat and bring to a simmer. Add the green beans and mangetout (snow peas), along with the frozen or tinned lotus root, if using, then simmer for 2 minutes until the green veg starts to get nice and tender. Add the Chinese broccoli, spinach, chard or pak choi (bok choy) and stir for 20 seconds, until they start to wilt.

Take the pan off the heat and add the coconut milk, along with more stock or boiling water if needed; the mixture should be soupy and silky smooth from the coconut milk. Mix well and season with tamarind pulp (or concentrated paste), and salt to taste. Set aside.

Fill a small saucepan with boiling water and place over a high heat. Boil the noodles for 2 minutes, then drain well.

Divide the noodles between 2 large bowls and ladle the curry broth on top. Squeeze half a lime over each bowl. Drizzle with a little chilli oil and scatter with chopped peanuts, if using, then dive into a mellow yellow world of curry-flavoured comfort.

● **Tip:** If you're using fresh lotus root, don't be intimidated – it's as easy as peeling a potato. Peel the outside, then slice the root into finger-width pieces. It's a beautiful little veggie that you'll fall in love with and use over and over again.

Green Curry Noodles with Chicken (Gaeng Keow Wan Gai)

Lean, Green Spice Machine

You've probably tasted many different versions, now you have your own authentic, super healthy, recipe. The fresh herbs make a vibrant, aromatic sauce, while the kaffir lime leaves, lime juice and fish sauce balance the sour and the salty for a marvellously mouth-filling flavour. The paste keeps for at least a week in the fridge, or even longer in the freezer.

400g (14oz) fresh thick yellow noodles, or 120g (4¼oz) dried thick yellow noodles
1 tablespoon vegetable oil
250g (9oz) chicken breasts or thighs, skinned and diced, or pork loin, thinly cut (or use tofu or mock chicken for a vegan alternative)
85g (3oz) green beans, trimmed
85g (3oz) baby corn
½ small carrot, peeled and sliced at an angle
300ml (½ pint) boiling water
2 tablespoons Mr Lee's Healthy Mussel Sauce (page 24) or ready-made fish sauce (or use Mr Lee's Vegan 'Fish' Sauce, page 25, or light soy sauce for a vegan alternative)
8 tablespoons good-quality coconut milk
½ teaspoon sea salt, or to taste
large handful of finely chopped fresh coriander (cilantro)
freshly sliced green chillies (optional), to serve

FOR THE CURRY PASTE:
1 teaspoon ground cumin
1 teaspoon ground coriander
4–8 green bird's-eye chillies, depending on how hot you want it
1 small red onion, peeled
1 heaped teaspoon garlic paste or 3 garlic cloves, peeled
1 tablespoon ginger paste, or 3cm (1¼in) piece of fresh root ginger, peeled
2 lemongrass stalks, ends trimmed and outer layer removed, or 2 teaspoons ground dried lemongrass
4 kaffir lime leaves, fresh, frozen or dried

large handful of fresh coriander (cilantro), including stems
large handful of fresh Thai basil, or use regular basil with a pinch of ground aniseed

To make the green curry paste, place all the ingredients in a food processor and blend together until smooth. That's it! You can then freeze it, or store in a clean jar in the fridge for up to a week.

If you're using dried noodles, half-fill a medium saucepan with boiling water and place it over a high heat. Add the noodles and simmer for 2 minutes until softened. Then drain well and set aside until needed.

Heat the vegetable oil in a large wok over a medium heat and add the curry paste. Let it gently fry for 2 minutes, releasing those fragrances and warming up the flavours. Add the chicken or pork pieces (or vegan alternative, if using) and stir-fry in the paste for 2–3 minutes, or until it is cooked on the outside. Then add the green beans, baby corn and carrot, along with the boiling water and mussel or fish sauce (or soy sauce if using), and bring to a simmer over a medium–high heat. Check the seasoning and add salt, or more soy or fish sauce, as you like.

Next, add the noodles and coconut milk, stirring well to combine everything. Increase the heat to high and stir-fry the soupy noodles for 1 minute, adding 2–4 tablespoons of water to loosen it up if you think it needs it. Add the final large handful of fresh chopped coriander (cilantro), mix well and remove from heat.

Divide the noodles between 2 large serving bowls. Scatter over some fresh coriander (cilantro) leaves and green chillies, if you like. Then kick back and imagine you're listening to the waves and some classic Moby (other vegan electro geniuses are available) in a ramshackle beach café while the sand tickles your toes. At least, we hope it's the sand – it had better not be a crab. Wait, we're the ones imagining this…OK.

- Serves 2
- A Little Effort
- Wok to wonderful in 30 minutes
- Hero ingredient: coconut milk (page 22)

Red Curry Noodles with Duck (Kaeng Phet)

Duck's Best Friend

If green curry is fragrant and punchy, red curry is its rich, earthy cousin. The shrimp paste in this recipe gives you the classic deep, salty umami flavour notes, which beautifully complement the duck. The red chillies bring a rich heat to the party, while the crunchy veg and the sweet pop of cherry tomatoes round it all out nicely.

½ tablespoon vegetable oil

250g (9oz) duck breasts, thinly sliced, skin removed

1 heaped tablespoon Mr Lee's Red Curry Paste (page 29)

6–7 spears of fresh asparagus, or a handful of green beans, fresh or frozen

10 cherry tomatoes

200ml (7fl oz) stock or water

2 generous tablespoons good-quality coconut milk

juice of ½ lime

1 teaspoon Mr Lee's Healthy Mussel Sauce (page 24) or ready-made fish sauce

1 teaspoon soy sauce

pinch of salt, to taste

400g (14oz) fresh egg noodles, or 120g (4¼oz) dried medium–thick egg noodles

½ fresh red chilli, finely sliced (optional)

Heat the vegetable oil in a wok over a medium–high heat. Add the duck pieces and stir-fry for 2 minutes, then add the curry paste and stir-fry for another 30 seconds. Mix it all up really well so those flavours get all over the duck. Stir-fry for another minute. Next add the asparagus (or beans, if using) and cherry tomatoes, and mix well over the heat.

Add the stock or water and bring to a simmer, then reduce the heat to medium and cook gently for 2 minutes. Remove the pan from the heat and add the coconut milk and lime juice. Stir gently, then add the mussel or fish sauce and soy sauce, and salt, if you like, to taste.

Half-fill a small saucepan with boiling water and place it over a high heat. Add the noodles, simmering for 1½ minutes if fresh and 2–3 minutes if dried.

Place the noodles in a bowl and pour the duck curry over the top. Top it off with extra red chillies if you like, and dive in.

- Serves 1
- Doddle / <15 Min / One-Wok Wonder / Vegan / Gluten-Free Option
- Wok to wonderful in 15 minutes
- Hero ingredient: walnuts (page 21)

Glass Noodles with Walnuts & Chilli

Train Food, But Not As You Know It

A classic Thai train station dish, you'll find sellers wandering down the platform with these spicy delights for weary, hungry travellers. You can forget your soggy cheese sarnie: if you're training it in Thailand, you eat well. It's the teeny tiny Thai red chillies that give this dish its kick, but the sour sauce and sweet agave mellow it out and take the edge off.

40g (1½oz) dried mung bean (glass) noodles
1 tablespoon walnut halves, roughly chopped
1 tablespoon vegetable oil
½ tablespoon agave syrup
1 tablespoon soy sauce
1 teaspoon Mr Lee's Vegan 'Fish' Sauce (page 25)
1–2 dried bird's-eye chillies, soaked, or use
    1 large fresh red chilli, finely sliced, to taste
pinch of sea salt, to taste
2 spring onions (scallions), finely sliced
½ tomato, diced
½ lime
¼ teaspoon ground white pepper
fresh coriander (cilantro) leaves, to garnish

Half-fill a saucepan with boiling water and place over a high heat. Add the noodles and cook for 5 minutes, breaking them up, then drain and plunge them into a bowl of cold water. Drain well and set aside.

Toast the walnuts in a dry wok or frying pan (skillet) over a medium heat for 1–2 minutes, stirring occasionally, until golden, then transfer to a plate and set aside.

Return the pan to the heat and increase the heat to high. Add the oil, followed by the agave, soy sauce, vegan fish sauce and chillies. Add a pinch of salt to taste. Cook for 1 minute, then throw in the noodles and toss well to coat with the dressing.

Next add half the walnuts, along with the spring onions (scallions) and tomato, and stir-fry for 1 minute 30 seconds over a very high heat. Pile the mixture on to a big serving plate.

Serve immediately, topped with the remaining walnuts, a squeeze of lime, a scattering of fresh coriander (cilantro) and a sprinkle of white pepper.

- Serves 2
- Doddle / One-Wok Wonder / Gluten Free Option
- Wok to wonderful in 30 minutes
- Hero ingredients: cinnamon and ginger (page 22)

Healthy Duck Noodle Soup (Ped Toon)
Deep Dish Duck

Hugely popular among Thai people but little known outside of Asia, Ped Toon is a special occasion dish. You'll often see it at festivals, with rows of duck-soup sellers surrounded by locals perched on plastic chairs, happily slurping their soup. Some sellers add cola to the broth for a little fizz and top it with shredded duck.

250g (9oz) duck breast, skinless
120g (4¼oz) dried yellow egg noodles, thin or thick, but you can use wheat noodles if you prefer
small handful of fresh bean sprouts, or small handful of finely sliced iceberg lettuce

FOR THE BROTH:
2 star anise, or a pinch of ground aniseed
½ tablespoon ground cinnamon
½ teaspoon Chinese five-spice powder
1 teaspoon ginger paste, or 2.5cm (1in) piece of fresh root ginger
1 teaspoon garlic paste, or 2 garlic cloves, crushed and chopped
½ teaspoon sea salt
1 teaspoon finely ground black pepper
1 tablespoon dark soy sauce
1 tablespoon light soy sauce
½ tablespoon Mr Lee's Healthy Mussel Sauce (page 24), or ready-made fish sauce
1 tablespoon honey or agave syrup
900ml (1½ pints) boiling water

FOR THE TOPPINGS:
small handful of fresh coriander (cilantro), roughly chopped
1 spring onion (scallion), finely chopped
1 tablespoon fried crispy garlic or onions (optional)

Put all the broth ingredients into a medium-sized saucepan over a medium–high heat and add the duck breast.

Cover with a lid and bring to the boil, then simmer over a medium heat for 20 minutes. Then remove the cooked duck and strain the broth through a fine sieve into a separate saucepan. Set the strained broth and the cooked duck aside.

Half-fill a small saucepan with boiling water and place over a medium heat. Add the noodles and boil for 2–3 minutes, depending on the thickness of the noodle.

To assemble the dish, divide the noodles between two large bowls and top with the bean sprouts or lettuce. Slice the duck and place in the bowls. Reheat the broth, bringing it back to the boil, then pour it all over the noodles. Finally, scatter over the toppings and get stuck in immediately.

- Serves 2
- Doddle / <15 Min /
  One-Wok Wonder /
  Gluten-Free Option
- Wok to wonderful in
  15 minutes
- Hero ingredients: crayfish,
  lemongrass and ginger
  (pages 21–23)

Creamy Tom Yum Noodle Soup with Crayfish Tails

Hot. Sour. Smashing.

In Laos, this royal-style dish puts rice at the bottom of the bowl and tops it with river fish. In posh city restaurants, they make it with lush seafood. But that hit of lemongrass, kaffir lime and spicy little Thai chillies is always there.

400g (9oz) fresh or 120g (4¼oz) dried thin
  rice noodles
240g (8½oz) crayfish tails, or use tail-on
  king prawns (jumbo shrimp)
small handful of bean sprouts, or small handful
  of finely sliced iceberg lettuce

FOR THE BROTH:
½ tablespoon vegetable oil
1 heaped teaspoon dried shrimp, finely chopped
½ tablespoon dried chilli flakes
½ small red onion, finely chopped
1 lemongrass stalk, crushed and chopped,
  or 1 teaspoon dried ground lemongrass
1 tomato, roughly chopped
few sprigs of fresh coriander (cilantro), finely chopped
1 teaspoon dark tamarind paste, or 2 tablespoons
  tamarind pulp/sauce (see page 18)
2 anchovy fillets, finely chopped
1 teaspoon ginger paste, or 2cm (¾in) piece
  of fresh root ginger, finely chopped
1 teaspoon garlic paste, or 2 garlic cloves,
  crushed and chopped
2 kaffir lime leaves, fresh, frozen or dried
1 tablespoon light soy sauce (or use tamari for
  a gluten-free alternative)
2 tablespoons Mr Lee's Healthy Mussel Sauce
  (page 24) or use ready-made fish sauce
1 tablespoon honey or agave syrup
100ml / 3 ½fl oz coconut cream
900ml (1½ pints) boiling water

FOR THE TOPPING:
few sprigs of fresh coriander (cilantro), roughly chopped
½ lemon or lime
1 large red chilli, roughly chopped
2–4 tablespoons evaporated milk or use coconut cream,
served on side (optional)

Begin by preparing the broth. Heat the vegetable oil in a large saucepan over a high heat. Add the chopped dried shrimp and chilli flakes and fry for just 5 seconds, then add all the broth ingredients to the pan and simmer for 5 minutes.

Meanwhile, half-fill a small saucepan with boiling water and add the rice noodles. Simmer for 2–3 minutes, depending on your preference, then drain.

Divide the noodles between 2 bowls and top with the bean sprouts or lettuce.

Bring the soup broth to a boil and add the crayfish. Cook for 10 seconds, then pour the broth all over the noodles.

Scatter the toppings over the noodles and serve immediately, with the coconut cream or evaporated milk on the side.

- Serves 2
- A Little Effort / <15 Min / Gluten-Free Option
- Wok to wonderful in 15 minutes
- Hero ingredient: chillies (page 20)

Beef & Prawns with Flat Rice Noodles

Thai-style Surf & Turf

Based on the popular dish 'Weeping Tiger' (Suea Rong Hai). The story goes that the tiger cried when the hunter came and took away its cow. Lots of questions here, like what was a tiger doing with a pet cow? Anyway, traditionally it uses brisket, but you can use fillet (tenderloin) steak for a leaner, succulent option. If you want to go gluten-free, swap out the soy sauce for tamari.

120g (4¼oz) dried Thai-style flat rice noodles, 4–6mm (1/8–¼in) wide
½ tablespoon vegetable oil
120g (4¼oz) fillet (tenderloin) steak or brisket, thinly sliced
1 large red chilli, or use 2 small Thai chillies, finely diced
1 large green finger chilli, finely diced
2 banana shallots, or 1 small red onion, roughly diced
85g (3oz) fresh or frozen king prawns (jumbo shrimp), raw, peeled
50g (1¾oz) bean sprouts
juice of ½ fresh lime (optional)
small handful of Thai basil, or use regular basil with a pinch of ground aniseed

FOR THE SAUCE:
2 tablespoons Mr Lee's Healthy Mussel Sauce (page 24) or ready-made fish sauce
2 tablespoons honey or agave syrup
2 tablespoons light soy sauce (or use tamari for a gluten-free option)
½ teaspoon ground white pepper

Soak the noodles in a large bowl of very warm water for 15–20 minutes depending whether you like them soft or chewy. Drain and set aside.

Mix together half of the diced chillies with half of the sauce ingredients in a small bowl and set aside for a pour-on sauce.

Heat the oil in a large wok over a super high heat. Throw in your beef, the remaining half of the red and green chillies, shallots or onion and king prawns (jumbo shrimp). Stir-fry for 45 seconds.

With the heat still high, add the bean sprouts, rice noodles, the remaining half of the sauce ingredients, and white pepper, mix well and stir-fry everything for another 2 minutes.

Sprinkle with the lime juice, then pile on to a large plate. Scatter over the basil and serve with the dressing sauce on side.

● Serves 2

● Showing Off /
Vegan Option /
Gluten-Free Option

● Wok to wonderful in
30 minutes

● Hero ingredients: green
jackfruit, lemongrass,
turmeric and ginger
(pages 21-22)

Khao Soi with Green Jackfruit

Mile High Curry

Chiang Mai is the gateway to the lush, mountainous north. After a hard day's trekking, there's nothing like returning to this comfortingly creamy and tangy noodle curry. The name means 'cut rice', but it could also come from the Burmese word for noodle, 'Khao Swe'. It blends traditional Thai red curry paste with the more earthy aromatic spices from neighbouring Burma and the northern spice routes.

2 tablespoons vegetable oil (optional)

10g (¼oz) dried rice vermicelli noodles (optional)

120g (4¼oz) dried egg noodles (or use egg free yellow noodles for vegan option)

FOR THE CURRY BROTH:

1 Chinese dried mushroom, or use 1 dried or fresh shiitake mushroom

2 large red chillies, finely chopped

½ small red onion, finely chopped

1 lemongrass stalk, ends trimmed and outer layer removed, or 1 teaspoon ground dried lemongrass

1 teaspoon ground cumin

½ teaspoon ground cinnamon

few sprigs of fresh coriander (cilantro), finely chopped

1 tablespoon mild or medium curry powder

½ tablespoon ground turmeric

1 teaspoon garlic paste, or 2 garlic cloves, crushed and chopped

1 teaspoon ginger paste, or 1cm (½in) piece of fresh root ginger, peeled and finely chopped

2 kaffir lime leaves, fresh or frozen (or use 3 dried leaves)

2 tablespoons light soy sauce (or use tamari for a gluten-free alternative)

1½ tablespoons agave syrup (or honey, if not vegan)

500ml (18fl oz) boiling water

560g (20 oz) tin young/green jackfruit, drained, rinsed and roughly chopped into pieces

400ml (14fl oz) good-quality coconut milk

FOR THE TOPPINGS

¼ small red onion, finely sliced

1 small gherkin, finely sliced

2 wedges of lime or lemon

½ red chilli, finely sliced

small handful of fresh coriander (cilantro), including stems, finely chopped

If you want to make crispy vermicelli noodles as a topping, heat the vegetable oil in a small frying pan (skillet) over a high heat. Add the rice vermicelli noodles and shallow-fry until crispy. Remove the noodles from the pan and place on a plate lined with paper towels. Set aside.

Place a medium-sized saucepan over a medium heat and add all the broth ingredients, except the coconut milk. Bring to the boil and simmer for 15 minutes over a medium heat.

 Now stir the coconut milk into the mixture and bring it back to boil, then take off the heat immediately and set aside.

Half-fill a small saucepan with boiling water and place over a high heat. Add the egg or yellow noodles and cook for 2–3 minutes, depending on whether you like 'em chewy or soft. Drain well and then divide between 2 bowls.

Pour the soup broth all over the noodles. Scatter the toppings over the noodles, along with the fried vermicelli, and serve immediately.

- Serves 2
- Showing Off / <15 Min / Gluten-Free / Vegan
- Wok to wonderful in 12 minutes
- Hero ingredient: garlic (page 20)

Spicy Thai Salad with Celeriac & Noodles (Som Tam)

From Laos with Love

You'll find this gorgeously sweet and salty salad in every street market and home in Thailand. This dish is originally from Laos, which has an incredibly wide array of food influences. It's usually made with green papaya, but that can be difficult to get hold of, so we've used celeriac (celery root).

120g (4¼oz) dried rice vermicelli noodles
1–4 red bird's-eye chillies (depending on how hot you want it), thinly sliced, or use ½–2 teaspoons chilli paste
1½ teaspoons garlic paste, or 3 garlic cloves, peeled and left whole
¼ celeriac (celery root), peeled and grated
½ small carrot, grated
small handful of green beans, trimmed and cut into 2.5 cm (1in) pieces
5 cherry tomatoes, quartered
2 tablespoons Mr Lee's Healthy Mussel Sauce or Vegan 'Fish' Sauce (page 25), or use ready-made fish sauce
2 tablespoons light soy sauce, or use tamari for gluten-free alternative
freshly squeezed juice of 1 lime
2 tablespoons agave syrup (or honey, if not vegan)
70g (2½oz) unsalted peanuts

Half-fill a small saucepan with boiling water and place over a high heat. Add the rice noodles and boil for 2 minutes, then drain and rinse with cold water to make sure they stop cooking and don't stick together. Set aside.

Grind the chillies and garlic a large pestle and mortar to make a paste, then set aside in a small bowl. If you don't have a pestle and mortar, you can also use a large plastic or metal bowl and grind and pound with the back of a large wooden spoon or rolling pin. It's a bit messy, but effective. If you've touched the chillies, remember to wash your hands! It could be an eye-watering experience if you don't.

Add the grated celeriac (celery root), carrot and beans to the mortar or large bowl and pound gently for 3–4 minutes, then throw in the cherry tomatoes and pound again for a few more minutes until the mixture is a bit mushy.

Then add the mussel or fish sauce (or vegan fish sauce), light soy sauce or tamari, lime juice and agave or honey, and keep pounding until the ingredients are nicely mixed. Return the chilli and garlic paste to the mortar and mix well. For a final flourish, add the noodles and peanuts, and mix well so all the noodles are well coated.

You can enjoy the salad immediately, or it'll keep in the fridge for up to 3 days. (Although, in all honesty, it'll probably be stolen. Not our fault – you've been warned.)

See picture overleaf (top left)

- Makes approx.
  14–16 pieces
- Little Effort /
  Gluten-Free Option
- Wok to wonderful in
  30 minutes
- Hero ingredient:
  lemongrass (page 21)

THAI

Thai-Style Mini Pork Burger Bites

The Perfect Party Platter Pile-up

Burger bites are a Western guilty pleasure, while this Thai-inspired healthy is just a pleasure. They're great piled on a platter for something different at a party. Dip them into some of our Mr Lee's house sauces for an extra hot, tangy or sweet hit. You can substitute the homemade hot sauce for shop-bought sriracha, and ready-made sweet chilli sauce is widely available.

20g (¾oz) dried rice vermicelli noodles
½ tablespoon vegetable oil

FOR THE BURGERS:
300g (10½oz) lean minced (ground) pork
½ small red onion, finely diced
½ lemongrass stalk, or ½ teaspoon ground
   dried lemongrass
2 small anchovies, finely chopped
1 teaspoon garlic paste, or 2 garlic cloves, crushed
   and finely chopped
½ teaspoon ground white pepper
1 teaspoon Mr Lee's Healthy Mussel Sauce
   (page 24) or use ready-made fish sauce
1 teaspoon light soy sauce (or use tamari for
   a gluten-free alternative)
1 tablespoon cornflour (corn starch)
1 teaspoon toasted sesame oil
1 teaspoon honey or agave syrup

TO SERVE:
40–80ml (1¼–2¾fl oz) Mr Lee's South East Asian
   Hot Sauce (page 24), or use sriracha
40–80ml (1¼–2¾fl oz) Andy's Quick Sweet Chilli
   Dip (page 25), or use shop-bought
lemon wedges

Place the noodles in a bowl of boiling water and leave to soak for 1–2 minutes. Drain well, then roughly chop them.

In a large bowl, mix together all the burger ingredients. Stir in the drained chopped noodles.

Using wet hands, form the meat mixture into golf-ball sized burgers and then flatten them a bit. Once you've formed your burger bites, place them on a board or tray, ready to cook.

Heat the vegetable oil in a large, wide frying pan (skillet) over a high heat. Add the burgers and cook for 2 minutes on each side, then reduce the heat to low and cook for a further 1 minute on one side only. Remove from heat and place on a plate lined with paper towels to drain any excess oil.

To serve, pile the burger bites on a serving plate, with lemon wedges and the dipping sauces in little bowls on the side. Then step back before the crowd descends. Head's up: they go fast.

 See picture overleaf (bottom right).

- Serves 2
- Doddle / One-Wok Wonder / Vegan / Gluten-Free
- Wok to wonderful in 20 minutes
- Hero ingredients: lemongrass and ginger (page 21/22)

Classic & Simple Thai Broth

Wake Up Your Taste Buds

Thai people will often have this for breakfast or as a light snack; you'll find it in any street market. It's the perfect pick-me-up. Traditionally flavoured with fish sauce, you can easily keep it plant-based and gluten-free using tamari. We like to put some pickled fresh chillies on the side to add a sour, spicy kick.

240g (8½oz) dried mung bean noodles, or use dried rice vermicelli noodles
½ tablespoon toasted sesame oil
½ tablespoon vegetable oil
2 teaspoons garlic paste, or 4 garlic cloves, crushed and chopped
1 tablespoon ginger paste, or 2.5cm (1in) piece of fresh root ginger
1 lemongrass stalk, crushed and chopped, or 1 teaspoon dried ground lemongrass
900ml (1½ pints) boiling water
1 teaspoon good-quality vegan bouillon powder, or soy bean paste
2 tablespoons tamari
½ teaspoon agave syrup
100g (3½oz) shredded white cabbage
100g (3½oz) shredded dark green cabbage or kale
1 carrot, coarsely grated, or cut into julienne strips
120g (4¼oz) bean sprouts
4 spring onions (scallions), sliced

TO SERVE:
2 small red Thai chillies, finely sliced (mixed with 45ml rice vinegar if you like – optional)
lime wedges
Mr Lee's Red Chilli Oil (page 29), optional

Place the noodles in a large bowl, fill with boiling water and leave for 10–15 minutes until the noodles are soft. Rinse, drain and set aside.

Heat the sesame and vegetable oils in a large saucepan over a low heat and fry the garlic until it starts to colour. Then add the ginger and lemongrass and cook for a further minute until the garlic is getting crispy.

Add the water and bouillon or soy bean paste and bring to the boil. Add the tamari and agave and simmer for 2 minutes.

Now add the shredded cabbage, carrot, bean sprouts, half of the chopped spring onions (scallions) and the noodles. Increase the heat to high and bring to the boil, then immediately remove from the heat.

To serve, pour into large, deep bowls. Top each bowl with the remaining spring onions (scallions), along with the chillies (in vinegar if you prefer) and a wedge of lime. Serve with Red Chilli Oil.

- Serves 2
- Doddle / <15 Min / One-Wok Wonder / Vegan Option
- Wok to wonderful in 15 minutes
- Hero ingredient: leafy greens (page 21)

Smoky Thai Fried Wide Noodles with Pork & Greens (Pad See Ew)

Sweet & Smoky Street-Food Superstar

This is all about layers of texture: smoky, charred noodles and caramelised pork . Typically, you'd use sen yai rice noodles. But use whatever you like. If you can't get Thai greens (pak kana) or Chinese broccoli, use any big leafy spinach, chard or pak choi (bok choy). Balance out the saltiness with Thai table sprinkles, like dried chilli flakes, chilli slices in rice vinegar, and honey.

220g (8oz) lean minced (ground) pork
  (or use vegan mince for a vegan alternative)
1 tablespoon vegetable oil
2 eggs (omit for the vegan option)
400g (14oz) fresh sen yai (or ho fun) flat,
  wide rice noodles
2 large handfuls of leafy greens, such as Thai greens
  (pak kana), Chinese broccoli (gai lan), or pak choi
  (bok choy), spinach, or chard, etc.

FOR THE MARINADE:
1 teaspoon garlic paste, or 2 garlic cloves, thinly sliced
½ teaspoon honey (or use agave syrup for
  a vegan alternative)
large pinch of ground white pepper
2 teaspoons Mr Lee's Healthy Mussel Sauce (page 24)
  or ready-made fish sauce (or use vegan fish sauce
  or light soy sauce for a vegan alternative)

FOR THE SAUCE:
1 tablespoon light soy sauce
1 tablespoon dark soy sauce
1 teaspoon agave syrup or honey
1 teaspoon ground white pepper
4 tablespoons water

TO SERVE:
1–2 teaspoons dried chilli flakes (optional)
1–2 teaspoons of agave syrup or honey (optional)
1–2 fresh green chillies, finely sliced, in
  2–3 tablespoons of rice vinegar (optional)

In a medium bowl, mix together the marinade ingredients until well combined. Then add the mince and mix well. Set aside for a few minutes to marinate. In another bowl, mix together all the sauce ingredients and set aside until needed.

Heat ½ tablespoon of the vegetable oil in a large wok over a medium–high heat. Add the marinated mince and fry for 5–6 minutes, stirring constantly, until completely cooked. Tip on to a plate, including any juices, and set aside.

Rinse the wok with water and wipe it clean, then place it over a smoking-hot high heat and add the remaining ½ tablespoon oil. Add the eggs (if using), breaking them into the wok, then push them to the side of the wok as they cook. Now add the noodles, spreading them wide across the wok so they char up a bit. Throw in the greens and stir-fry everything, still on a super-high heat, for another 30 seconds.

Add the cooked mince and stir-fry for a further 30 seconds, then add the sauce and cook for 30 seconds more. If it starts to dry up, add a splash of water.

Pile the noodles on to 2 plates, and serve immediately alongside some agave or honey, chilli flakes and chillies. Freshly sliced green chillies in vinegar are a traditional accompaniment and well worth it. Just add a few tablespoons of rice vinegar to a small bowl of finely sliced green chillies. As with pad Thai, you can use these accompaniments to adjust the levels of spicy, sour and sweet to suit your taste.

See picture on previous spread (bottom left).

Korean food has gone global in recent years; most cities have at least one great Korean barbecue joint. You'll never forget your first Korean fried chicken sandwich, dripping with chilli sauce, kimchi slaw and deliciousness . . . Give us a minute, we're having a bit of a moment here.

Korean food rocks some truly unique flavours that you won't find anywhere else. They've pretty much reinvented the barbecue, or bulgogi as they call it, with soy, sesame and fresh Asian flavours. And then there's the kimchi pickle. Kimchi is in that tiny category of foods that both taste amazing and are ridiculously good for you. It's one of the most naturally healing foods you can eat. And don't get us started on the deep, umami-rich soups, the pillowy buns, crispy pancakes and fritters, or we'll be here all day.

Korean food is for sharing: it's a way for people to come together. So you'll find a lot of sharing platters and food that's made for groups. You usually have a big main noodle (myeon) or rice (bap) dish, but it's the accompaniments and side dishes that put Korean food into a league of its own. A dazzling range of pickles, pastes, pancakes and dips. Sometimes hot, sometimes cold. Sometimes spicy, sometimes mellow. They bring a whole world of textures and flavours to every dish. At Mr Lee's, we think Korean food is a game-changer and we've put together a selection of go-to noodle recipes that make exploring this foodie world healthy, easy and super-tasty.

5

Korean

Marinated Beef with Kimchi Udon Noodles

Rain or Shine Anytime Barbecue

Korean barbecue's (bulgogi) soy, sesame and open flame combo is an absolute winner. Use a 'hot as you dare' cast-iron grill pan to scratch that BBQ itch without messing around with coals. We've added kiwi to the marinade to tenderise the meat and save some time. The classic smoky, spicy flavours of Korean barbecue play so well with the stir-fry and bouncy udon noodles.

250g (9oz) beef sirloin (porterhouse) or rib-eye, fat removed, thinly sliced into approx. 10 slices

400g (14oz) fresh udon noodles, or use 120g (4¼oz) dried thick spaghetti

1 tablespoon vegetable oil

115g (4oz) Mr Lee's Super Simple Kimchi (page 26), or good-quality ready-made kimchi

2 spring onions (scallions), finely sliced

FOR THE MARINADE:

¼ kiwi, peeled and very finely chopped

½ onion, thickly sliced

½ tablespoon ginger paste, or 3cm (1¼in) piece of fresh root ginger, grated

1 teaspoon garlic paste, or 2 garlic cloves, crushed and chopped

1 tablespoon light soy sauce

1 teaspoon honey or agave syrup

1 teaspoon toasted sesame oil

¼ teaspoon sea salt

½ teaspoon ground white pepper

FOR THE STIR-FRY SAUCE:

2 teaspoons light soy sauce

2 teaspoons Korean red pepper paste (gochujang)

2 teaspoons honey or agave syrup

1 teaspoon toasted sesame oil

Mix all the marinade ingredients together in a big bowl and add the beef slices. Make sure they're well coated so they soak up the marinade flavours. Set aside for at least 15 minutes.

Meanwhile, put your feet up and enjoy a cold beer – or you could use the time to throw together some little Korean sides, like super-fast sesame pickled Korean veg (page 173) or soy and braised daikon (page 170). It's your party, we won't judge either way. If you're using dried spaghetti, you can also use this time to cook the spaghetti according to the packet instructions, then drain and set aside until needed.

When you're ready to cook, place a wide, flat frying pan (skillet) or cast-iron griddle pan over a very high heat. Lightly grease with ½ tablespoon of the vegetable oil. If you're using cast iron, let that pan get hot, hot, hot!! When it's as hot as it'll get, add the beef, gently shaking off the excess marinade as you lift the pieces out of the bowl. Leave the onion slices in the marinade bowl. Fry the beef for 30 seconds over this very high heat, then turn the pieces and fry for another 30 seconds. Add 1–2 tablespoons of the remaining marinade to the pan and mix it all up. Remove the beef pieces and set aside on a plate to rest.

In a small bowl, mix together the stir-fry sauce ingredients.

Heat the remaining oil in a wok over a high heat and fry the fresh udon noodles or drained cooked spaghetti. After 30 seconds, add the stir-fry sauce mixture, along with the remaining marinade (including the onions) and kimchi. Stir-fry for a further 45 seconds, then remove the wok from the heat.

Divide the noodle mixture between 2 big bowls, or pile it up on one big serving platter. Place the beef pieces on the top of the stir-fried noodles, scatter with the spring onions (scallions) and enjoy your faff-free barbecue!

Seafood Ramyeon with Korean Red Pepper

Ramen with a Korean Makeover

A Korean take on a Japanese favourite. We're bringing some spicy, pungent gochujang to the party. Gochujang dances to its own tune; it's unlike any other chilli paste. Sometimes labelled red pepper paste, look out for it in Asian supermarket. When you combine this with the sweet scallops and prawns, the umami-rich mushrooms and the cabbage, it gives ramen a spicy Korean makeover.

140g (5oz) dried ramen noodles, or dried wheat and/or egg noodles
120g (4¼oz) scallops
120g (4¼oz) raw fresh prawns (shrimp), or any seafood, e.g. squid or cooked mussels
1 tablespoon Korean red pepper paste (gochujang)
½ tablespoon vegetable oil
60g (2¼oz) fresh shiitake or chestnut mushrooms, sliced
60g (2¼oz) savoy cabbage, finely sliced
¼–½ teaspoon sea salt
¼ teaspoon ground white pepper
2 teaspoons light soy sauce
1 teaspoon smoked paprika powder
1 teaspoon toasted sesame oil
1 tablespoon finely chopped spring onion (scallion), to serve

Place a small saucepan of boiling water over a high heat and add the noodles. Boil for 3 minutes, then drain well and set aside.

Place the scallops and prawns (shrimp) – or whatever seafood you're using – in a small bowl. Add ½ tablespoon of the gochujang and mix it all together, using your hands to coat everything really well.

Next heat the vegetable oil in a wok over a very high heat and add the seafood to the pan. Fry for 45 seconds, keeping the heat super high so the seafood caramelises and gets golden brown around the edges.

Add the mushrooms and cabbage and lightly season with the salt and pepper. Stir everything well, cooking for a further 45 seconds.

Finally add the cooked and drained noodles to the wok, along with the soy sauce, paprika, sesame oil and remaining gochujang. Stir-fry for another 2 minutes, over a high heat, combining everything well. Add a tablespoon or two of water to loosen the sauce.

Divide the noodles between 2 serving bowls and sprinkle with the spring onion (scallion) – cheffy flourish is optional. Serve immediately.

- Serves 2
- Doddle / One-Wok Wonder / Vegan Option / Gluten Free Option
- Wok to wonderful in 25 minutes
- Hero ingredients: anchovies, shiitake mushrooms, seaweed and kimchi (pages 20–23)

Fermented Soy Bean Paste Noodle Soup (Doenjang Jjigae)

Food to Fall in Love to

This beloved stew is said to hold the key to a Korean man's heart. So you can forget about matching onesies: apparently the stew will do it. Even if your intentions are strictly platonic, this dish is still a winner. It's all built around the rich, deep flavours of doenjang (fermented soy bean paste; see page 17). It's a bit like miso, but more so!

120g (4¼oz) dried rice vermicelli noodles

2 jarred anchovies, finely chopped (or, for a vegan alternative, use 1½ tablespoons vegan fish sauce, page 25, or 2 tablespoons light soy sauce and 1 teaspoon good-quality vegan bouillon)

1 tablespoon doenjang (Korean fermented soy bean paste), or use red or brown miso paste

½ teaspoon garlic paste, or 1 small garlic clove, crushed and chopped

½ teaspoons Korean red chilli flakes (gochugaru), or use ¼ teaspoon mild chilli powder and ¼ teaspoon smoked paprika

750–800ml (1¼–1½ pints) boiling water

pinch of dried seaweed, such as wakame or dulse (optional)

180g (6¼oz) firm tofu, diced into small cubes, or use lean cooked turkey breast if you prefer

1 courgette, chopped into bite-sized pieces

45g (1½oz) fresh shiitake mushrooms, or use chestnut or oyster mushrooms, thickly sliced

1 spring onion (scallion), sliced, white and green parts separated

½ teaspoon roasted sesame oil

½ teaspoon light soy sauce (or use tamari for a gluten-free option)

pinch of ground white pepper

TO SERVE:

2–4 tablespoons Mr Lee's Super Simple Kimchi (page 26), or good-quality ready-made kimchi, or super-fast sesame pickled Korean veg (page 173)

45g (1½oz) enoki mushrooms

1 large red chilli, finely sliced into strips

Place a small saucepan of boiling water over a medium–high heat. Add the noodles and cook for 4 minutes, then drain and set aside.

Place a large wok over a medium–high heat and add the chopped anchovies. Cook for 10–15 seconds, then add the doenjang, garlic and chilli flakes, and stir-fry for another 20 seconds, mashing it all up. Now add the boiling water and, using a whisk or fork, blend the paste well until it's nice and smooth.

Bring the broth to a simmer over a medium heat and add the seaweed, tofu (or turkey), courgette, shiitake mushrooms, spring onion (scallion) whites, sesame oil and soy sauce or tamari. Season with the white pepper and simmer for 2 minutes. Add the rice noodles, mix well and simmer for a further minute. Then remove from the heat.

You can divide the stew between 2 bowls or, if you want to put on a show, bring the wok to the table with a big ladle and a few accompanying sides, such as the kimchi or sesame pickled veg. Top the stew with some roughly torn enoki mushrooms, the spring onion (scallion) greens and the fresh chilli strips. Then go make someone fall in love with you!

- Serves 2
- A Little Effort
- Wok to wonderful in 30 minutes
- Hero ingredient: goji berries, ginger and buckwheat (pages 20-23)

Chicken Noodle Soup with Pear, Yam & Goji Berries

Korean Comfort Food

Every culture has its own version of a chicken soup. This leaves you with an 'Everything's going to be OK' glow. But with a Korean twist. So it's sweet, savoury and light. The little Korean pears bring some lovely sweetness and tenderise the meat, but if you can't get your hands on them, use normal pears and adjust the weight a bit (normal pears are smaller).

280g (10oz) chicken breasts, skinless, cut into thick strips

40g (1½oz) fresh Chinese yam, peeled and thinly sliced, or 30g (1oz) dried yam

1 large pear (approx. 120g/4¼oz), peeled, deseeded and sliced into strips

1 tablespoon ginger paste, or 2.5cm (1in) piece of fresh root ginger, peeled and finely diced

½ teaspoon garlic paste, or 1 garlic clove, crushed and finely chopped

900ml (1½ pints) boiling water, or ready-made fresh chicken bone broth

90g (3¼oz) dried soba noodles, or 120g (4¼ oz) dried jajang noodles, or any dried ramen noodles

1–1½ tablespoons goji berries

1 tablespoon Mr Lee's Healthy Mussel Sauce (page 24), or ready-made fish sauce

FOR THE DIPPING SAUCE:
2 tablespoons light soy sauce
½ teaspoon chilli oil
¼ teaspoon sesame oil

Place the chicken, yam, pear, ginger and garlic in a deep saucepan and add the boiling water. Place over a medium–high heat and bring to a fast simmer. Cook, uncovered, for 15 minutes.

Meanwhile, place a small pan of boiling water over a medium heat and add the noodles. Cook for 5 minutes, then drain well and divide the noodles between 2 big serving bowls.

Add the goji berries to the chicken pan and simmer for another 5 minutes, then finish the soup by adding the mussel or fish sauce. Mix well and remove from the heat.

Make the dipping sauce by mixing the ingredients together in a small cup or bowl. Pour the chicken and soup over the noodles and serve immediately, with the bowl of dipping sauce on the side, so you can dunk the chicken pieces into the nutty, spicy sauce. It'd be rude not to!

- Makes 2 – Serves 1 as main, or 2 as starter
- Showing off / vegetarian
- Wok to wonderful in 30 minutes
- Hero ingredients: kimchi and spirulina (page 22/23)

Pancake Tacos with Kimchi Salsa

Korea to LA, via Mexico

Grab your passport, we're flying from Korea to LA via Mexico. We love tacos and we love Korean food, so let's put them together! The spirulina gives them a cool blue–green colour. The kimchi gives some spicy tanginess to the salsa and brings a party atmosphere to the savoury egg-dipped tofu. This fabulous fusion treat is packed with protein, healthy fats and fermented goodness.

15g (½oz) dried mung bean noodles, or any dried rice noodle
1 large egg
1 heaped tablespoon plain flour
½ teaspoon spirulina powder
¼ teaspoon sea salt
1 tablespoon water
85g (3oz) firm tofu, diced into 1cm (½in) cubes
½ tablespoon light soy sauce
1 tablespoon vegetable oil
1 spring onion (scallion), finely sliced
small handful of bean sprouts or shredded iceberg lettuce, to serve

FOR THE KIMCHI SALSA:
2 tablespoons Mr Lee's Super Simple Kimchi (page 26) or ready-made kimchi
2.5cm (1in) piece of cucumber, deseeded and diced into 0.5cm (¼in) cubes
½–1 large red chilli, finely chopped, to taste (optional)

FOR THE DRESSING:
1 teaspoon light soy sauce
½ teaspoon toasted sesame oil

Start by soaking your noodles in a bowl of freshly boiled water for 10 minutes, then drain and set aside.

Separate the egg between two bowls.

To the egg-white bowl, add the flour, spirulina, salt and 1 tablespoon of water, beating with a fork or whisk to make a thick batter. Add another tablespoon of water if the batter seems too thick. Set aside.

Next lay the tofu pieces on a plate and drizzle with the soy sauce, moving the pieces around to season each one. Beat the egg yolk, pour it over the tofu and mix well.

Heat ½ tablespoon of the vegetable oil in a small frying pan (skillet) over a medium heat. Working in batches of 4 or 5 pieces, carefully place the eggy tofu into the pan. Lightly fry each batch for 1 minute, turning several times until the egg coating is cooked and golden. Place the cooked tofu on a plate lined with paper towel to drain any excess oil. Set aside, ready to fill the tacos.

In a small bowl, mix together the kimchi salsa ingredients. In another small bowl or jug, combine the dressing ingredients.

Wipe the frying pan you used for the tofu with some paper towel, then use it to heat the remaining ½ tablespoon oil over a medium–high heat. Once hot, scatter half the spring onion (scallion) and half the noodles across the pan so the base of the pan is evenly covered. Let them cook for 1 minute, then pour half the batter over the top, using a spoon to smooth over the noodles and fill in any gaps. Fry for 2–3 minutes until golden brown, then turn over and cook for another 2 minutes. Remove from the pan and set aside, then repeat with the remaining noodles, spring onion and batter to make a second pancake.

To serve, lay each pancake taco on a plate and scatter with some bean sprouts or shredded lettuce. Lay some tofu pieces on top. For a final flourish, top with some kimchi salsa and drizzle with the soy-sesame dressing.

Mr Lee's Korean Club Sandwich

Yeah, We Went There

We've taken this room-service classic and given it some Korean love. Spicy gochujang goes so beautifully with the velvety mayo, and we've punched up the chicken and lean bacon with some smoky Korean goodness. Lighter, spicier – dare we say better? Yes, we do. We believe this is the ultimate club sandwich. If you disagree, please email all complaints to chilloutitsonlyasandwich@mrleesnoodles.com

180g (6½oz) chicken breast fillet, sliced lengthways to make 2 thin escalopes
1 teaspoon Korean red pepper paste (gochujang)
¼ teaspoon sea salt
4 back bacon slices, any excess fat trimmed
½ teaspoon Korean red chilli flakes (gochugaru), or use ¼ teaspoon mild chilli powder and ¼ teaspoon smoked paprika
1 tablespoon vegetable oil
6 slices mini rice noodle cake, or use brown bread slices if you can't find these unusual noodles
½ teaspoon maple syrup or honey
handful of lamb's lettuce, or other fresh salad leaves

FOR THE OMELETTE:
½ tablespoon vegetable oil
1 egg
1 tablespoon grated mature hard cheese
½ tablespoon sliced spring onion (scallion) greens
pinch of sea salt

FOR THE GOCHUJANG MAYO:
1 tablespoon Korean red pepper paste (gochujang)
2 tablespoons good-quality mayonnaise
¼ teaspoon ground black pepper
¼ teaspoon toasted sesame oil (optional)

FOR THE KIMCHI TOMATO RELISH:
1 large ripe tomato, diced
2 tablespoons Mr Lee's Super Simple Kimchi (page 26), or ready-made kimchi, finely chopped
¼ teaspoon toasted sesame oil

Place the chicken pieces in a small bowl with the gochujang paste and salt. Using your hands, mix it all up to make sure it's well coated. Place the bacon in another bowl and add the gochugaru chilli flakes and maple syrup or honey. Mix well and set aside for a few minutes.

Heat ½ tablespoon of the vegetable oil in a large frying pan (skillet) over a high heat. Lay the noodle cakes into the pan and fry on each side until golden brown and crispy on the outside. Set aside. If using bread, you can lightly toast if you like.

Add the remaining ½ tablespoon vegetable oil to the pan and place over a medium heat. Add the marinated chicken and cook for 3 minutes on each side. Then add the marinated bacon to the pan and cook on each side for 1 minute. Remove the pan from the heat and place the chicken and bacon on a plate to rest.

Wipe the pan clean with a paper towel, ready to make the omelette. Heat ½ tablespoon vegetable oil in the pan over a medium heat. In a small bowl, beat together the egg, cheese and spring onion (scallion) greens, along with a pinch of salt. Pour the mixture into the pan and fry for 1–2 minutes, turning once, to make a small omelette. Remove from the heat, then lay the omelette on a plate lined with paper towels to drain any excess oil. Slice the omelette into four pieces, each approximately 5 x 7.5cm (2 x 3in).

Make the gochujang mayo by mixing together the ingredients in a cup or small bowl, whisking with a fork to blend well. Set aside.

Make the tomato kimchi relish by mixing together the tomato, chopped kimchi and sesame oil in a small bowl or cup.

OK, let's build our sandwich. Take 2 serving plates, and place 1 noodle cake on each one. Begin to stack the sandwich by adding the omelette layer, followed by some salad leaves. Drizzle with a little of the gochujang mayo, then place the chicken on top. Top with one noodle cake, then add another layer of omelette, followed by the bacon and more salad leaves onto this second layer. Drizzle with more gochujang mayo. Top off with a final noodle cake, and serve with the tomato kimchi relish on the side, as well as any leftover mayo.

Mr Lee's Osam Bulgogi with Braised Daikon

Squiddy, Porky Perfection

Osam is short for ojingeo-samyeopsal (squid and pork belly) – you can see why we shortened it! This is our healthy, 30-minute Korean banquet. The braised daikon side dish adds a whole new flavour dimension. We've upped the quantities for the braised daikon to make twice as much as you need because it's a gem of a side and also keeps for ages.

120g (4¼oz) dried sweet potato noodles, or use thick mung bean noodles
½ tablespoon vegetable oil
130g (4½oz) pork loin, thinly sliced
¼ teaspoon ground black pepper
½ tablespoon garlic paste, or 2 garlic cloves, crushed and chopped
½ tablespoon ginger paste, or 3cm (1¼in) piece of fresh root ginger, peeled and finely chopped
115g (4oz) Mr Lee's Super Simple Kimchi (page 26) or ready-made kimchi, plus extra to serve
½ large red bell pepper, thinly sliced
½ large red onion, thinly sliced
1 large red chilli, finely chopped
130g (4½oz) squid, sliced into bite-sized pieces, including tentacles, or use fresh or frozen calamari rings if you prefer, sliced in half
1 spring onion (scallion), finely chopped
1 tablespoon toasted sesame seed

FOR THE BRAISED DAIKON:
½ daikon (Asian radish), approx. 150g (5½oz), cut into 0.5cm (¼in) slices
2 tablespoons light soy sauce
1 tablespoon honey or agave syrup
½ tablespoon toasted sesame seeds
250–300ml (9–10fl oz) water

FOR THE STIR-FRY SAUCE:
1 tablespoon Korean red pepper paste (gochujang)
½ tablespoon Korean red chilli flakes (gochugaru), or use 1 teaspoon mild chilli powder and ¼ teaspoon smoked paprika

1 tablespoon light soy sauce
½ tablespoon honey or agave syrup
150ml (¼ pint) water
½ tablespoon toasted sesame oil

To make the braised daikon, add all the ingredients to a small saucepan. Place the pan over a medium heat and get it simmering. Cook for 25 minutes uncovered, until the sauce is almost completely reduced and the radish has softened slightly. Set aside.

Now place a small saucepan of boiling water over a medium–high heat. Add the sweet potato noodles and simmer for 7 minutes, then drain and set aside.

Mix together all the stir-fry sauce ingredients in a small bowl or cup and set aside until needed.

Heat the vegetable oil in a large frying pan (skillet) over a high heat and add the pork. Stir-fry for 1 minute and season with the black pepper. Add the garlic and ginger and cook for 10 seconds. Then add the kimchi, red bell pepper, red onion and chilli, stir-frying for another 10 seconds.

Finally, it's squid time! Add the squid, along with the stir-fry sauce mixture and drained noodles. Bring everything up to a simmer and cook for a further 10–15 seconds. Once everything is cooked, pour into a large serving platter or bowl, sprinkling with spring onions (scallions) and toasted sesame seeds. Serve immediately alongside the braised daikon, and extra kimchi if you like.

- Serves 2
- A Little Effort / Vegetarian / Gluten Free Option
- Wok to wonderful in 25 minutes
- Hero ingredients: sesame seeds/ oil and shiitake (page 20/22)

Japchae Sweet Potato Noodle Salad

Sweet 'n' Savoury Super Soaker

These chewy sweet potato noodles are brilliant at soaking up flavours. Hugely popular in Korea, japchae is traditionally eaten with beef on special occasions – you'll find it in just about every Korean restaurant. It goes with any protein, but we've kept ours veggie with mushrooms. Serve your japchae with Mr Lee's Super Simple Kimchi (page 26), super-fast sesame pickled Korean veg (page 173) and braised daikon (page 170).

120g (4¼oz) fresh shiitake mushrooms, sliced
120g (4¼oz) dried sweet potato noodles
¼ teaspoon rice vinegar
2 eggs
½ tablespoon vegetable oil
1 carrot peeled and cut into 5cm (2in) matchsticks
pinch of sea salt
1 onion, brown or red, thinly sliced
½ red bell pepper, thinly sliced
1 large handful of Chinese spinach, roughly chopped, or use fresh watercress or baby spinach

FOR THE MARINADE:
1 teaspoon light soy sauce
1 teaspoon toasted sesame oil
¼ teaspoon ground black pepper

FOR THE DRESSING:
1 tablespoon light soy sauce
1 tablespoon toasted sesame oil
½ tablespoon toasted sesame seeds

In a medium bowl, mix together the ingredients for the marinade. Add the sliced mushrooms, combine well and set aside for a couple of minutes.

Meanwhile, place a small saucepan of boiling water over a medium–high heat and add the noodles. Boil for 7 minutes. Once cooked, use a slotted spoon or tongs to lift the noodles out of the pan and into a sieve or colander, leaving the noodle water in the pan. Using scissors, quickly cut the noodles into shorter strands, around a quarter of the original length.

Keeping the noodle water over a medium–high heat, add the rice vinegar and crack the eggs into the rolling boiling water. Cook for 2–3 minutes, depending on how soft you prefer the yolk.

While the eggs are cooking, heat the vegetable oil in a wok over a high heat. Throw in the carrots, along with a pinch of salt, and stir-fry for 1 minute. Next, add the mushrooms and stir for another minute. Then add the onion and red bell and cook for another 45 seconds, stirring well. Set aside.

Transfer the cut noodles into a large mixing bowl and add the spinach or watercress, along with the contents of the wok. Mix it up really well.

In a small bowl or jug, mix together the dressing ingredients.

Divide the noodle mixture between two bowls and place a poached egg on top of each one. Finish with a generous drizzle of the dressing, and dive in.

- Serves 2
- A Little Effort / Vegetarian / Vegan Option
- Wok to wonderful in 25 minutes
- Hero ingredients: sesame seeds and shiitake (page 20/22)

KOREAN

Korean Black Bean Noodles with Vegetables (Jajangmyeon)

Takeaway with a Twist

The Brits have fish and chips; Koreans have jajangmyeon. It was probably brought by the Chinese a century ago, and over the years it has been perfected to become South Korea's favourite takeaway dish. Look for thick, chewy noodles labelled jajangmyeon or chunjang/chajang/jajang. You can find them in most east Asian grocery shops. But if you can't, use udon noodles, or even thick spaghetti.

½ tablespoon vegetable oil

½ courgette, cut into 1–2cm (½–¾in) dice

½ carrot, cut into 1–2cm (½–¾in) dice

handful of green beans, trimmed and cut into 2cm (¾in) pieces

4–5 fresh shiitake mushrooms, cut into 1–2cm (½–¾in) dice

1 tablespoon Korean black bean paste (chunjang)

1 tablespoon agave syrup

220ml (8fl oz) boiling water

1 tablespoon toasted sesame oil

400g (14oz) fresh or 120g (4¼oz) dried jajang noodles, or use fresh udon noodles or dried thick spaghetti

FOR THE SUPER-FAST SESAME PICKLED KOREAN VEG:

10cm (4in) piece of fresh cucumber, peeled and finely sliced

¼ teaspoon sea salt

½ red pepper, finely sliced

½ teaspoon Korean red chilli flakes (gochugaru), or use ½ teaspoon mild chilli powder and ¼ teaspoon smoked paprika

½ teaspoon garlic paste, or 1 small garlic clove crushed and chopped

2 teaspoons rice vinegar

1 teaspoon agave syrup or honey

1 teaspoon toasted sesame seeds

Begin with the quick-pickled vegetables. Add the prepped cucumber to a small bowl and sprinkle with the salt. Mix well and set aside for 5–10 minutes, then rinse and pat dry using some paper towel. Add all the other pickle ingredients to a mixing bowl and mix it all together, Then add the cucumber and combine so everything is well coated. Cover and set aside. Job number one done!

Heat the vegetable oil in a wok over a very high heat. Add the courgette, carrot, green beans and mushrooms and stir-fry for 1 minute.

Pour over the black bean paste and agave and combine well, stir-frying for another minute. Add the boiling water and sesame oil, mix well, then remove from the heat.

Place the noodles in a small pan of boiling water and cook for 30 seconds if fresh, and 3½ minutes if dried. (If you're using spaghetti, or a different type of noodle, cook according to the packet instructions.) Drain well. Divide the noodles between two bowls, then pour the contents of the wok all over the top. Serve immediately with a side of pickled vegetables. Super South Korean takeaway, and not a foil tray in sight.

See picture overleaf (bottom left).

• Serves 2   • Showing Off   • Wok to wonderful in   • Hero ingredient:
                                              30 minutes   sesame seeds and
                                                                              ginger (page 20/22)

Korean 'Fried' Sticky Chicken

The Colonel's Got Nothing on This

Korean fried chicken is a global street-food phenomenon. This Mr Lee's healthy makeover gives you that crunchy Korean fried chicken hit without the greasy comedown. We've covered the whole thing in a moreishly tangy sauce. Seriously, you could put this stuff on cardboard and it'd be gorgeous. (Note from Mr Lee's lawyers: Please do not put the sauce on cardboard and eat it.)

See picture on previous spread (top right)

1 teaspoon light soy sauce

1 teaspoon toasted sesame oil

1 teaspoon garlic paste, or 2 garlic cloves, crushed and finely chopped

250g (9oz) chicken thighs, boneless and skinless, cut into strips approx. 2–3cm (¾–1¼in) wide and 3–4cm (1¼–1½in) long

8 tablespoons Korean breadcrumbs (ppanggaru), or use Japanese panko breadcrumbs

½ tablespoon self-raising flour

1 egg

3 tablespoons vegetable oil

120g (4¼oz) dried jajang noodles, or ramen noodles

¼ cucumber, deseeded and cut into 5cm (2in) batons

FOR THE CHICKEN MARINADE:

1 tablespoon light soy sauce

1 tablespoon Korean red pepper paste (gochujang)

½ tablespoon sesame oil

1 tablespoon toasted black sesame seeds, or use white

FOR THE POUR-OVER DRESSING:

½ tablespoon Korean red pepper paste (gochujang)

1 tablespoon dark soy sauce

2 tablespoons honey or agave syrup

1 teaspoon ginger paste, or use 1.5cm (⅝in) piece of fresh root ginger, peeled and finely chopped

½ tablespoon lemon juice

Put the light soy sauce, sesame oil and garlic into a medium bowl and mix it all up well. Then add the chicken strips and mix, coating the chicken. Set aside for 5 minutes.

Now heat the vegetable oil in a wide frying pan (skillet) over a medium–high heat with 3 tablespoons of vegetable oil. While it's heating, pour the breadcrumbs on to a small plate. Add the flour to the chicken mixture and mix. Then add the egg to the chicken mixture and mix, again so the chicken is completely coated. With one hand, take a piece of marinated chicken, letting any excess drip off, then roll it in the dry breadcrumbs to coat. Take your dry hand, dip the piece back into the batter, and then back into the breadcrumbs. Lay the piece of chicken straight into the hot pan, and repeat with the other pieces of chicken.

Fry the breaded chicken for 3–5 minutes on each side, or until golden brown. When you turn the chicken, start with the first pieces you put into the pan, so they all get evenly cooked (you can check by cutting into a thick piece with a knife). Once the chicken pieces are cooked, place them on a plate with paper towel to absorb any extra oil.

Meanwhile, place a small saucepan of boiling water over a medium heat. Add the noodles and boil for 5 minutes, then drain well. Place the drained noodles into a mixing bowl and add the sauce ingredients, mixing it all up nicely. Divide the noodles between 2 serving plates. Add the chicken pieces and cucumber batons.

Mix together the dressing ingredients in a small bowl and pour over the noodles, and you're done. Don't be shy, get stuck in!

- Serves 2
- A Little Effort / Vegan
- Wok to wonderful in 25 minutes
- Hero ingredient: sesame seeds (page 20)

Korean Spring Onion Noodle Pancakes (Pa-Jeon)

Any Time, Any Way Pancakes

Street food has been at the centre of Korean life for over 600 years, so you'll often see people strolling down the road, munching on these hand-held treats. Serve with the healthy, tangy, sweet and spicy dip, and, if you're going down the sharing route, add a few extra sides, like kimchi (page 26) or super-fast sesame pickled Korean veg (page 173).

35g (1¼oz) dried sweet potato noodles
½ tablespoon vegetable oil
3–5 spring onions (scallions) trimmed and halved lengthways

FOR THE BATTER:
50ml (2fl oz) ice-cold water
2 tablespoons self-raising flour
2 tablespoons cornflour (corn starch) or potato starch
1 tablespoon light soy sauce
½ teaspoon doenjang (Korean fermented soy bean paste), or use brown or red miso paste
1 teaspoon toasted sesame seeds

FOR THE DIPPING SAUCE:
½ tablespoon agave syrup (or honey, if not vegan)
½ tablespoon light soy sauce
½ tablespoon lemon or lime juice
½ tablespoon toasted sesame seeds
½ teaspoon finely sliced red chilli
½ teaspoon garlic paste, or 1 garlic clove, crushed and finely chopped
1 teaspoon toasted sesame oil (optional)

Place a small saucepan of boiling water over a medium–high heat and add the noodles. Boil for 7 minutes, then drain well and roughly chop with scissors.

Meanwhile, mix together the batter ingredients in a large mixing bowl. Add the chopped noodles and stir to combine.

In a small bowl, mix together the dipping sauce ingredients and set aside.

Heat the vegetable oil in a non-stick frying pan (skillet) over a medium heat. Place the spring onions (scallions) into the pan and sauté for 15–20 seconds, then pour the batter mixture into the pan. It should form a thin layer over the top of the spring onions. You can use a spatula to smooth it out if needed. Fry gently for 3 minutes or until golden brown, then carefully turn over (flip it if you're feeling lucky!) and cook for a further 3 minutes. Use spatula to flatten the pancake down, by constantly pushing it lightly. Once cooked and golden brown, remove from heat.

Chop the pancake ready to serve – it is traditionally sliced with diagonal cuts, making diamond-shaped bite-sized pieces to share and dip at the table. Serve the pancake alongside the dipping sauce and your chosen side dishes.

See picture on previous spread (top left)

Kimchi Mandu with Pork & Mung Bean Noodles

Dumplings to Die For

These tasty little parcels of Korean loveliness can be steamed or pan-fried if you like a crispy bottom. Mandu (or Mandoo) means 'dumpling' in Korean. You can buy ready-made dumpling wrappers in any Asian supermarket. Wrapping dumplings with loved ones is a special bonding experience in many Asian cultures, so get ready for some dumpling love. OK, that just sounds wrong.

12 round mandu dumpling pastry sheets
½ tablespoon vegetable oil
handful of plain flour for dusting

FOR THE FILLING:
20g (¾oz) dried mung bean or green bean noodles
150g (5½oz) kimchi, roughly chopped
100g (3½oz) lean minced (ground) pork
1 teaspoon light soy sauce
1 teaspoon Mr Lee's Healthy Mussel Sauce (page 24), or ready-made fish sauce
1 teaspoon honey or agave syrup
2 tablespoons cornflour (corn starch) or potato starch
½ teaspoon sesame oil

FOR THE DIPPING SAUCE:
2 tablespoons light soy sauce
1 tablespoon any kind of vinegar, or lime juice
½ teaspoon honey or agave syrup
½ teaspoon chilli oil
½ teaspoon finely sliced garlic

Before you begin, line a tray with greaseproof paper (baking parchment).

Soak the mung bean noodles in a bowl of freshly boiled water for 5 minutes, then drain and finely chop.

Place the chopped noodles in a large bowl and add all the other filling ingredients. Mix well to thoroughly combine.

Open out your pastry sheets, laying on to a lightly floured work surface, and cover them with a damp cloth, keeping them covered so they don't dry out.

To make a dumpling, place a teaspoon of the filling mixture in the centre of one of the pastry sheets. Moisten the edges of the sheet with water and fold the pastry in half until it has covered every part of the mixture, making a ball shape in the centre. Pinch and fold the edges together to seal the dumpling. Place the dumpling on to the lined tray and repeat with the remaining pastry sheets and filling. Once you've made all your dumplings, place them in the freezer for 30 minutes before cooking.

When you're ready to cook, heat the vegetable oil in a large, non-stick frying pan (skillet) over a medium heat. Pop the dumplings into the pan and fry them on both sides until they're firm and a little translucent. Add a large splash of boiling water to the pan, to a depth of about 2cm (¾in), half covering the dumplings. Cover with the lid and cook for 3 minutes.

Meanwhile, mix all the dipping sauce ingredients together in a small bowl and set aside.

Remove the lid and turn the dumpling over to cook on the other side. Increase the heat up high and let the water reduce. When the dumplings turn crispy and golden, they're ready to be devoured with the lovely sweet and tangy dipping sauce.

'Army Base' Stew with Cheesy Turkey Escalope, Sausage & Beans (Budae-Jjigae)

A Warming Bowl of History. And Sausages.

The Korean War was a time of serious food scarcity: you made the most of what you had. And in Korea, they made something beautiful. Sweet and spicy, this one-pot wonder is named after the army stew. Army surplus dishes like spam, hot dogs and baked beans bulk it out. Times have changed, but this is still a hugely popular dish all over Korea.

1 teaspoon toasted sesame oil

2 lean hot dog sausages, sliced on an angle into bite-sized pieces

140g (5oz) turkey breast, sliced lengthways to make long, thin fillet strips

1 teaspoon garlic paste, or 2 garlic cloves, crushed and chopped

½ small onion, finely chopped

1–1½ tablespoons Korean red pepper paste (gochujang), depending on how spicy you like it

115g (4oz) Mr Lee's Super Simple Kimchi (page 26) or ready-made kimchi, plus extra to serve

120g (4oz) dried ramen or wheat noodles

2 small heads of pak choi (bok choy), or a large handful of spinach

2 slices of Edam or Leerdamer cheese, or other melting cheese of your choice

1 spring onion (scallion), finely sliced at angle

FOR THE BROTH:

600ml (20fl oz) boiling water

1 tablespoon good-quality chicken or vegetable stock powder, or 3–4 small jarred anchovies

4 large or 6 small dried shiitake mushrooms, cut in half with scissors if large

½ tablespoon Mr Lee's Healthy Mussel Sauce (page 24), or ready-made fish sauce

1 tablespoon Korean red chilli flakes (gochugaru), or use ½ tablespoon mild chilli powder and ½ teaspoon smoked paprika

1 tablespoon mirin

½ tablespoon honey or agave syrup

¼ teaspoon ground black pepper

65g (2½oz) canned haricot beans, drained and rinsed, or healthy, low-sugar baked beans (optional)

Heat the sesame oil in a large saucepan over a medium–high heat. Add the sausages and gently fry for a couple of minutes, or until they just start to brown. Then add the turkey breast strips and lightly fry for 30 seconds on each side. Next bring the garlic, onion, gochujang and kimchi to the party. Let them mingle and stir-fry for another 30 seconds.

In a large jug, mix together all the broth ingredients, stirring well to combine. Now pour the stock mixture over everything in the pan and simmer for 5 minutes, covered, to let the flavours intensify.

Take the pan off the heat and tuck the dried noodles into the middle of the pot, topping up with a little more water, if needed, to make sure everything is covered. Tuck the pak choi (bok choy) heads or spinach into any gaps around the side. Replace the lid and return to the heat, simmering for 3 minutes. Then remove the lid and lay the cheese slices over the noodles. Take the pan off the heat and cover with the lid for 45 seconds until the cheese goes all gooey and melts on to the noodles.

Take the dish to the table, ladling the stew into small bowls, alongside extra kimchi and sprinkle with sliced spring onion if you like.

In many ways, Vietnamese cuisine is the world's first fusion food. There's nowhere else in the world where you'll find dishes influenced by India, Japan and France – sometimes all on the same plate. And yet, even though Vietnamese food is influenced by all of these amazing foodie countries, it is also beautifully its own thing. The hero ingredient is their fish sauce, Nước mắm. It's made from fermenting anchovies in plankton-rich waters, and is pretty much the taste of Vietnam. You'll also find roasted peanuts, sour, tangy tamarind and fat green bunches of fresh herbs in a lot of Vietnamese dishes. Vibrant is the word that sums it all up.

In the north, you'll find big Chinese influences with the subtly spiced and herby dishes that make the most of dried fish, preserves and pickled vegetables. In the south, the beautiful produce from the Mekong Delta is brought to vibrant life by Indian spices. French and Japanese influences also pop up all over the place.

Ho Chi Minh is a modern metropolis, packed with high-end restaurants and innovative street food stalls pushing Vietnamese cuisine into the future. Meanwhile, in Hanoi, centuries-old architecture and a lively café culture spill out on to the streets in a wave of multicoloured tables, chairs, irresistible aromas, bubbling pots and slurping diners. All while physics-defying traffic weaves in and out of the tasty chaos.

On this noodle journey, you'll experience the rich diversity of influences that make Vietnam's vibrant food so wonderful.

6

Vietnamese

- Serves 2
- A Little Effort
- Wok to wonderful in 30 minutes
- Hero ingredients: cinnamon and ginger (page 22)

Phở bò

The Big Boy from Hà Nội

If you're ever in Hanoi, follow your nose and you'll drift into a star anise- and cinnamon-spiced wonderland. Tiny, multi-coloured clusters of plastic stools and low tables packed with happy diners hunched over big bowls of piping hot phở (pronounced 'fuh'). It's the combination of the chewy noodles and the tender beef (bò) swimming in a richly spiced, warming broth that makes it.

175g (6oz) dried flat rice noodles, 2–4mm ((¹⁄₁₆–(¹⁄₈in) wide
200g (7oz) beef fillet (tenderloin), thinly sliced

FOR THE BROTH:
½ tablespoon of vegetable oil
2 onions, finely diced
½ tablespoon ginger paste, or use ½ thumb of fresh ginger, peeled & finely chopped
225g (8oz) lean minced (ground) beef (unless you're using ready-made bone broth)
900ml (1½ pints) good-quality beef bone broth or 900ml (1½ pints) boiling water
½ tablespoon garlic paste, or use 3 cloves of fresh garlic, peeled, crushed & finely chopped
2 whole star anise
5cm (2in) cinnamon stick, or a large pinch of ground cinnamon
2 green cardamom pods, or a small pinch of ground cardamom
2 cloves
1–2 tablespoons Mr Lee's Healthy Mussel Sauce (page 24), or ready-made fish sauce
½ teaspoon sea salt, to taste
½ teaspoon finely ground white pepper
½ apple, peeled and finely sliced

FOR THE TOPPINGS:
1 spring onion (scallion), finely sliced
80g (2¾oz) bean sprouts
2 tablespoons deep-fried shallots or onions (optional)

a small handful each of roughly torn fresh herbs, including mint, coriander (cilantro), Vietnamese or Thai basil, or European basil
1–2 tablespoons Mr Lee's South East Asian Hot Sauce (page 24), Mr Lee's Red Chilli Oil (page 29) or use ready-made sriracha
1–2 tablespoons Mr Lee's Hoisin Sauce (page 25)
½ lime or lemon, or you can use a few drops of orange juice

Begin by making the broth. Place a medium-sized saucepan over a medium–high heat and add the vegetable oil plus the onions and ginger, stir-frying for 2-3 minutes until slightly coloured and fragrant.

If you're using ready-made bone broth, add it now, followed by the rest of the broth ingredients.

If you're using minced (ground) beef and water, add the beef now, mixing it up until it's nicely browned. Then throw in all the other ingredients except the water. Keep stirring for 2–3 minutes, then add the boiling water.

Cover the pan with a lid, reduce the heat to low and leave to simmer for 20 minutes, as your kitchen starts to smell like downtown Hanoi (in a good way!).

Meanwhile, half-fill another medium saucepan with boiling water and place over a medium heat. Add the dried noodles and simmer for 3–4 minutes. Drain well and divide the noodles between 2 large deep soup bowls. (Give yourself a bit more if you like – we won't tell, and you did do all the cooking.)

Add the uncooked sliced beef fillet / tenderloin on top of the noodles. Then use a fine sieve to strain the broth over the noodles in each bowl.

Garnish with a flourish, scattering over the spring onion (scallion), bean sprouts, deep-fried shallots and fresh herbs, and adding hoisin sauce, chilli sauce or red chilli oil and a squeeze of fresh citrus to taste. For an authentic Hanoi experience, grab yourself a plastic chair that's way too small and dive in!

Vietnamese Broth served with Cuttlefish Patties & Fresh Greens (Bún chả)

Soupy Street-food Goodness

Everyone's mum makes the best bún chả. It's truly loved in Vietnamese homes and on the street-food stalls of Hanoi. Bún chả are round rice noodles served with a broth and various meats, greens and herbs (bún means 'noodle' in Vietnamese). A vibrant selection of pickles and dipping sauces take things to the next level. Every bite is a different flavour adventure.

100g (3½oz) dried rice vermicelli noodles
1–2 teaspoons vegetable oil

FOR THE CUTTLEFISH PATTIES:
200–250g (7–9oz) fresh cuttlefish, finely chopped, or use minced (ground) chicken or pork, if you prefer
¼ teaspoon ground white pepper
¼ teaspoon dried chilli flakes
1 teaspoon cornflour (corn starch) or potato starch

FOR THE DIPPING SAUCE:
1 tablespoon rice vinegar
2 tablespoons honey or agave syrup
1 tablespoon light soy sauce (use tamari for a gluten-free option), Mr Lee's Healthy Mussel Sauce (page 24), or ready-made fish sauce
½ tablespoon finely chopped red chilli
1 teaspoon garlic paste, or 2 cloves of garlic, finely chopped
1 tablespoon freshly chopped coriander (cilantro) stems
250ml (9fl oz) water

FOR THE SALAD:
50g (1¾oz) bean sprouts
70g (2½oz) iceberg, romaine or baby gem lettuce
small handful of fresh coriander (cilantro)
a few mint leaves
85g (3oz) cucumber, thinly sliced

Place all the cuttlefish patty ingredients into a large bowl and mix together – stir in one direction for 1 minute and the mixture will come together. Then shape the mixture into 8–10 bite-sized patties and set aside until needed.

Place a small saucepan of boiling water over a medium–high heat. Add the noodles and simmer for 4–5 minutes, then drain and set aside in a serving bowl.

In a small bowl, mix together the dipping sauce ingredients and set aside until needed.

In a large bowl, mix together the salad ingredients and set aside until needed.

Heat the vegetable oil in a frying pan (skillet) over a high heat. Add the patties and fry for 1½ minutes on each side. Remove from the pan and place on a plate lined with paper towel to drain any excess oil.

Now arrange your serving platter. Place the dipping sauce bowl in the centre, then pile up the noodles, the herby salad and the patties around the outside.

- Serves 2
- A Little Effort / <15 Min / Vegan Option
- Wok to wonderful in 15 minutes
- Hero ingredients: peppercorns, lemongrass, anchovies and coconut water (pages 21-23)

VIETNAMESE

Chicken & Lemongrass Noodle Soup with Green Peppercorns

Comfort with Added Zing!

Chicken and lemongrass…is there anything else that's simultaneously vibrant and soothing? Most chicken noodle soups nail the comfort factor: they're like a warm blanket. But this Vietnamese take brings a little zing to the party, too. It's more like a cape. Still comforting, but also stylish and cool. Capes are cool, aren't they?

240g (8½oz) chicken or turkey breast, sliced into bite-sized pieces (or use mock chicken for a vegan alternative)
½ tablespoon vegetable oil
100g (3½oz) dried egg noodles (or use dried egg-free yellow noodles for a vegan alternative)

FOR THE MARINADE:
1 lemongrass stalk, ends removed, crushed and finely chopped
¾ tablespoon Mr Lee's Healthy Mussel Sauce page 24, or ready-made fish sauce (or Mr Lee's Vegan 'Fish' Sauce on page 25 for a vegan alternative)
large pinch of freshly ground black pepper
fresh lime or lemon, to serve
Mr Lee's Red Chilli Oil (page 29), or freshly sliced red chillies, to serve

FOR THE BROTH:
1 small anchovy fillet, finely chopped (omit for vegan option)
1 lemongrass stalk, ends removed, crushed and finely chopped
1–2 tablespoons fresh green peppercorns, or any fresh peppercorns, or use dried
5–6 cherry tomatoes, quartered
1 teaspoon garlic paste
400ml (14fl oz) boiling water, or use ready-made fresh chicken or vegetable broth

400ml (14fl oz) coconut water (100 per cent pure, no added sugar)
1 tablespoon Mr Lee's Healthy Mussel Sauce page 24, or ready-made fish sauce (or use Mr Lee's Vegan 'Fish' Sauce, page 25, for a vegan alternative

Place all the marinade ingredients in a large bowl and mix together really well. Then add the chicken (or mock chicken) and mix until well-coated. Set aside for 5 minutes.

Heat the oil in a wok over a high heat. Add the chicken (or mock chicken) and fry for 3 minutes on each side. Remove and set aside to rest on a plate.

Use the same wok to make the broth. Reduce the heat to medium, add the anchovy and fry for 30 seconds. Add the lemongrass, peppercorns, tomato and garlic and stir-fry over a medium heat for 1 minute. Then pour in the boiling water or broth and simmer for a further 5 minutes, letting those flavours bubble and intensify.

Meanwhile, place a small pan of boiling water over a medium–high heat and add the noodles. Cook them for 2–3 minutes. Once the noodles are soft, drain well and divide between 2 serving bowls.

To finish the soup, add the coconut water and fish sauce, then bring it back to a simmer. Pour the soup over the noodles, placing the chicken (or mock chicken) pieces on top. Serve with wedges of fresh lime or lemon, and red chilli oil or freshly sliced red chillies.

- Serves 2
- A Little Effort / Vegan
- Wok to wonderful in 30 minutes
- Hero ingredients: buckwheat and ginger (page 20/22)

Cao Lầu Hội An Noodles with Five-spice Tofu & Crispy Wonton

A Big Bowl of History

This famous dish comes from the picture-perfect ancient port town of Hội An. It's a vibrant mix of architectural eras and styles, from wooden Chinese temples to colourful French colonial buildings. Showcasing China's five-spice influence, it's best served cold with some wonton crackers (super-easy to find in the supermarket) and the warm sauce poured over the top.

2 tablespoons vegetable oil

3 pieces of wonton pastry, each cut into 4 small squares

250g (9oz) firm smoked tofu, or use any firm tofu

100g (3½oz) soba noodles

100g (3½oz) bean sprouts

5–6 Little Gem lettuce leaves, or use iceberg
   or another lettuce

small handful of watercress or lamb's lettuce (optional)

pinch or two of dried chilli flakes, or use ½ fresh
   red chilli, finely sliced

few sprigs of fresh mint, roughly torn

FOR THE SAUCE:

1 teaspoon vegetable oil

½ teaspoon ginger paste, or 1.5cm (⅝in) piece
   of fresh root ginger, peeled and finely chopped

½ teaspoon garlic paste, or 1 small garlic clove,
   crushed and chopped

1 small banana shallot or ½ small onion, finely chopped

3 tablespoons sake

2 tablespoons agave syrup (or substitute honey
   if not vegan)

2 tablespoons dark soy sauce

1 tablespoon light soy sauce

1 star anise

¼ teaspoon Chinese five-spice powder

200ml (7fl oz) boiling water

Heat the vegetable oil in a small frying pan (skillet) over a high heat. Add the wonton pastry and shallow-fry until it's nice and crispy. Then remove it and lay it on a plate lined with paper towel to soak up any oil.

To make the sauce, wipe out the excess oil from the pan and place it over a medium heat, adding the 1 teaspoon vegetable oil, followed by the ginger, garlic and shallot. Now throw in the rest of the sauce ingredients, mixing well.

Now add the tofu and reduce the heat to a simmer for 5 minutes. Carefully turn the tofu over and cook for a further 5 minutes. Remove the pan from the heat. Once it's cooled down, remove the tofu from the pan and slice it into 1cm (½in) thick wedges. Set aside. Keep the remaining sauce in the pan to pour over at the end.

Meanwhile, place a small saucepan of boiling water over a high heat and add the soba noodles. Boil for 3 minutes, then drain well. Divide the bean sprouts between 2 bowls, then place the drained noodles on top. Tuck the lettuce leaves and watercress or lamb's lettuce around the sides and lay the tofu slices on top, then drizzle over the remaining sauce from the pan. For a final flourish, add the crispy wonton pastry pieces and serve immediately with some fresh chilli or dried chilli flakes and a scattering of mint.

- Serves 2
- A Little Effort / <15min / Vegan Option / Gluten-Free Option
- Wok to wonderful in 15 minutes
- Hero ingredient: coconut water (page 22)

Vietnamese Chicken Salad with Rice Noodles (Gỏi Gà)

Looks Good, Feels Good

A hidden gem from south Vietnam, this is a technicolour delight of orange, red, green and white. We're seeing this little beauty pop up all over the world, but it's really big in Da Nang, Vietnam's third largest city. We've packed the flavourful salty, sweet and spicy dressing, known as nước chấm, with nutrient-rich coconut water and honey. A big bowl of colourful goodness!

50g (1¾oz) dried rice vermicelli noodles

100g (3½oz) bean sprouts

½ orange carrot, grated

½ purple or yellow heritage carrot, peeled and grated (optional)

200g (7oz) white cabbage or romaine lettuce hearts, shredded

½ small red onion, finely sliced

200g (7oz) cooked shredded rotisserie chicken, breast or thighs, skin removed (or use vegan mock chicken for a vegan alternative)

FOR THE DRESSING:

150ml (¼ pint) coconut water (100 per cent pure)

1 tablespoon finely chopped fresh mint

½–1 large red chilli, finely chopped

1½ tablespoons Mr Lee's Healthy Mussel Sauce (page 24), or ready-made fish sauce (or Mr Lee's Vegan 'Fish' Sauce, page 25, for a vegan alternative)

juice of ½ lemon

zest of ¼ lime

1 tablespoon honey (or agave syrup for a vegan alternative)

¼ teaspoon ground white pepper

¼ teaspoon sea salt

TO SERVE:

1 tablespoon chopped peanuts

a few sprigs of coriander (cilantro)

Soak the noodles in a bowl of freshly boiled water for 8–10 minutes, then drain. Roughly cut the noodles into smaller pieces with scissors.

Place the prepared noodles in a large mixing bowl along with the bean sprouts, carrot, cabbage or lettuce and onion. Mix it all up, then stir in the shredded cooked chicken (or mock chicken).

In a small bowl or jug, mix together all the dressing ingredients, then pour it over the mixture in the mixing bowl. Combine everything nicely so that the sauce coats all the salad ingredients. Pile it all into a large serving bowl and sprinkle with peanuts and a few coriander (cilantro) sprigs. Step back, admire the colours, then tuck in.

See picture overleaf (top left)

- Serves 2
- ● Doddle / Vegan / Gluten-Free Option
- ● Wok to wonderful in 25 minutes
- ● Hero ingredient: garlic (page 20)

VIETNAMESE

Braised Aubergine Clay Pot with Glass Noodles

Saucy little hotpot

This is real comfort food from the cooler northern regions. The clay pot may have originally come from China, but Vietnam makes this its own with fish sauce and freshly torn herbs. We've punched the sauce up with tangy tamarind and used our homemade vegan fish sauce to keep it plant-based. For true authenticity, use some nước mắm or vegan fish sauce.

225–250g (8–9oz) aubergine, peeled and sliced into 2–3cm (1–1.5in) slices

½ tablespoon vegetable oil, plus extra for brushing

100g (3½oz) dried mung bean (glass) noodles

½ teaspoon garlic paste, or 1 garlic clove, crushed and finely chopped

40g (1½oz) leek or onion, chopped into thick slices

180g (6½oz) courgette, chopped

½ tablespoon Mr Lee's Vegan 'Fish' Sauce (page 25, made with tamari for a gluten-free option), or use 1 teaspoon crushed yellow bean sauce or red miso paste

1 tablespoon light soy sauce (or use tamari for a gluten-free alternative)

1 tablespoon tamarind pulp (light brown) or use ½ teaspoon tamarind paste

300ml (½ pint) boiling water

¼ teaspoon freshly ground black pepper

¾ teaspoon cornflour (corn starch) mixed with 1 tablespoon water

2 tablespoons agave syrup (or use honey if not vegan)

½ large red chilli, finely sliced, to serve

few sprigs of fresh coriander (cilantro), to serve

Toss the aubergine pieces in vegetable oil. Then place in a large, non-stick frying pan (skillet) and fry the aubergine over a high heat for 3 minutes on each side. Once it's nicely browned and soft, lay the pieces on a plate and set aside.

Soak the noodles in a bowl of freshly boiled water for 8 minutes. Once they're soft, drain and place in a serving bowl or clay pot. Lay the aubergine pieces on top of the noodles.

Return the frying pan to a medium heat and add the ½ tablespoon vegetable oil. Add the garlic, onion and courgette, and stir-fry for 30 seconds. Next add the vegan fish sauce, soy sauce, tamarind and boiling water and season with the black pepper. Bring to a simmer for 30 seconds, then add the cornflour (corn starch) mixture to thicken, and sweeten with agave to taste.

Pour the sauce over the aubergine pieces and noodles, finish with a scatter of fresh chillies and coriander (cilantro), and dive in.

 See picture overleaf (top right)

Summer rolls with Crayfish Tails & Pickled Cabbage (Gỏi Cuôn)

Now THAT's a Wrap!

Not your greasy, deep-fried takeaway spring rolls. These are feathery light and packed with raw veggies, soft aromatic leaves and squidgy noods, all snuggled up in their rice wrapper. So many textures, so much flavour and goodness wrapped into every bite. We're using crayfish but you can pack these with pork, prawns, tofu, crunchy veggies, chicken; whatever you like.

20g (¾oz) dried rice vermicelli noodles
250–300g (9–10½oz) small crayfish tails
80–100g (2¾–3½oz) romaine lettuce
160g (5¾oz) cucumber, deseeded and cut into
    thin batons, 4cm (1½in) long
24 mint leaves, picked
24 Vietnamese or Thai basil leaves, or use
    European, picked (optional)
8 dried rice paper sheets (each approx.
    22cm/8½in in diameter)
lettuce leaves, to serve (optional)

FOR THE PICKLED CABBAGE:
150–200g (5½–7oz) white cabbage, finely shredded
1 tablespoon rice vinegar
½ tablespoon honey or agave syrup
½ teaspoon nước mắm (Vietnamese fish sauce),
    or use Mr Lee's Mussel Sauce (page 24) for
    a gluten free option
¼ teaspoon garlic paste, or ½ small garlic clove,
    crushed and finely chopped
¼ teaspoon freshly chopped red chilli

FOR THE DIPPING SAUCE:
2 tablespoons Mr Lee's Hoisin sauce (page 25)
½ tablespoon smooth peanut butter
½ teaspoon garlic paste, or use 1 small clove,
    crushed and finely chopped
½ tablespoon roasted peanuts, roughly chopped
    or crushed (optional)

 See picture on previous spread (bottom)

Begin by mixing all the pickle ingredients together in a bowl and set aside for 10 minutes.

Then, place a saucepan of boiling water over a medium heat and add the noodles. Cook for 3–4 minutes, drain and set aside.

Next, make the dipping sauce. In a small bowl, mix the hoisin sauce, peanut butter and garlic. Once it's all mixed, sprinkle the peanuts on top, if using.

Now divide your pickled cabbage, rice noodles, crayfish tails, lettuce, cucumber, mint leaves and basil leaves into 8 equal portions. You're making 8 rolls in total, so you want each portion to be a similar size.

When you're ready to roll, soak a rice paper sheet In warm water for 4–6 seconds. Don't worry about ripping it: rice paper is tougher than it looks.

Lay the paper on a chopping board, with the softer surface facing downwards and the rough side facing upwards. Now place a portion of lettuce on the side of the circle closest to you, followed by a portion of rice noodles, then of pickled cabbage and finally of cucumber. Try to cover each portion with the next, so you've a bit of everything in each bite.

Lift the side of the rice paper nearest to you, and roll it tightly towards the centre. Now arrange a portion of crayfish, and one of mint leaves (and basil, if using) in a line across the centre, from left to right. Fold the side ends in towards the middle, and tuck them in slightly, as though you're wrapping a parcel. Once the sides are tucked in, you can continue rolling to the end. Repeat until you've made all your rolls.

Serve the rolls either whole on lettuce leaves, or sliced in half at an angle and stacked on a plate – but always with a big bowl of the dipping sauce on the side.

- Serves 2
- A Little Effort / Vegan Option
- Wok to wonderful in 20 minutes
- Hero ingredient: lemongrass (page 21)

VIETNAMESE

Bánh Mì Baguette

Move over, Subway

The late, great Anthony Bourdain once described the bánh mì as a 'symphony in a sandwich'. Suck it, Subway! We're using lean pork paired with a crunchy, herby salad and a decadent slathering of Mr Lee's chilli sauce, all topped with crispy noodles and super-fast sesame pickled veg. For the authentic experience, pimp it up with layers of pâté or cheese!

250–280g (9–10oz) pork loin or chicken breast (or use firm tofu for a vegan alternative), cut into thin slices

½ tablespoon vegetable oil

small handful of dried mung bean noodles

2 small brioche or sandwich baguettes

1–2 tablespoons Mr Lee's South East Asian Hot Sauce (page 24), or ready-made sriracha

1–2 tablespoons smooth pâté of your choice, such as mushroom, crab or chicken (optional; choose a vegan pâté for vegan option)

1–2 tablespoons good-quality mayonnaise (optional; omit for vegan option)

1–2 triangles of cream cheese, such as Laughing Cow or DairyLea (optional; omit for vegan option)

¼ romaine heart lettuce

2 tablespoons super-fast sesame pickled Korean veg (page 173), or 1 small gherkin, finely sliced

handful of fresh herbs, such as mint, coriander (cilantro) and Thai basil

FOR THE MARINADE:

½ lemongrass stalk, ends removed, crushed and finely chopped, or ½ tablespoon ground dried lemongrass

¼ teaspoon chilli powder

1 tablespoon Mr Lee's Healthy Mussel Sauce (page 24), or ready-made fish sauce (or Mr Lee's Vegan 'Fish' Sauce for a vegan alternative, see page 25)

1 tablespoon honey (or agave syrup for a vegan alternative)

¼ teaspoon black pepper

1 teaspoon garlic paste, or use 2 garlic cloves, finely chopped

Place all the marinade ingredients in a large bowl and mix well to combine. Add the pork, chicken or tofu slices, making sure they're all nicely coated, then set aside for 10 minutes.

Meanwhile, heat the vegetable oil in a wok over a high heat. Add the mung bean noodles and shallow-fry until they crisp up. Transfer them to a plate lined with a paper towel and set aside.

Return the wok to the heat and add the marinated pork, chicken or tofu pieces. Stir-fry for 3 minutes. Take the pan off the heat and push the pork to one side in the wok. Leave to rest.

Slice the baguettes and lightly toast them under the grill (broiler) to your liking. To build a bánh mì, slather one side of a baguette roll with chilli sauce and some pâté if using, and the other side with mayonnaise and cheese, if using. Add some lettuce leaves, pickled veg and roughly torn fresh herbs, then layer the pork, chicken or tofu inside. Top with a little more chilli sauce, if you like, then sprinkle with the crispy noodles and serve. Serve with more chilli sauce on the side if you want to give it extra punch.

- Serves 2
- A Little Effort / Vegan Option / Gluten Free Option
- Wok to wonderful in 22 minutes
- Hero ingredients: turmeric, ginger, lemongrass and coconut water (pages 21-22)

Vietnamese Fish Curry with King Prawns (Cà Ri)

Creamy coconut cracker

Rich turmeric and coconut, tender flaky fish and sweet juicy prawns – is there anything better than a really good curry? Southern Vietnamese curries are heavily influenced by India, so you'll find lots of garam masala and other Indian spices playing a starring role. You can keep it plant-based by swapping the fish for veggies and tofu if you like.

80–100g (2¾–3½) dried rice vermicelli noodles
200g (7oz) haddock fillet, cut into approx. 6 pieces, or use hake, cod, coley or any firmer white fish, line-caught and local where possible (or use firm tofu for a vegan alternative)
100g (3½oz) raw tail-on king prawns (jumbo shrimp), or small sweet prawns or brown shrimp (see above for a vegan alternative)
1 tablespoon Mr Lee's Healthy Mussel Sauce (page 24), or ready-made fish sauce (or use light soy sauce for a vegan alternative, or tamari for gluten-free)
200ml (7fl oz) coconut milk
2–3 lemon or lime wedges
handful of fresh coriander (cilantro)
½ large red chilli, finely sliced

FOR THE BROTH:
½ tablespoon vegetable oil
½ onion, finely diced
2 tablespoons ginger paste, or a 4–5cm (1½– 2in) piece of fresh root ginger, peeled and finely chopped
1 teaspoon garlic paste, or 2 garlic cloves, crushed and finely chopped
1 lemongrass stalk, ends removed, crushed and finely chopped, or 1 tablespoon ground dried lemongrass
½ tablespoon annatto oil
½ tablespoon smooth peanut butter (optional)
600ml (20fl oz) coconut water (100 per cent pure, no added sugar)
1 tablespoon cornflour (corn starch) or potato or tapioca starch

4cm (1½in) piece of fresh turmeric root, peeled and finely chopped, or 1 teaspoon ground turmeric
½ tablespoon medium curry powder
½ teaspoon dried chilli flakes or chilli powder

Begin by preparing the broth. Heat the vegetable oil in a large saucepan over a medium heat. Add the garlic, onion, ginger and lemongrass, and stir-fry for 30 seconds.

Next add the annatto oil and the peanut butter and stir-fry for another 30 seconds, combining everything well. Mix a little coconut water with the cornflour or tapioca starch, making a paste, then stir into the mixture, along with the remaining coconut water and let it simmer for 2 minutes.

Then add the fish pieces and prawns if you're using big ones. Add the vegetables if using. Simmer gently for 3 minutes. If you're using small sweet or cooked prawns (or tofu), then just add them for the last minute.

Meanwhile, place a small saucepan of boiling water over a medium heat. Add the noodles and cook for 3–4 minutes, then drain well. Divide the noodles between 2 serving bowls. Add the mussel or fish sauce or soy sauce/tamari to the noodles, mixing slightly.

Add the coconut milk to the curry and take the pan off the heat. Stir gently, then carefully spoon the curry over the noodles. Serve with lemon or lime wedges, freshly sliced red chilli and a few coriander (cilantro) leaves. Now, crack open a beer – it's Curry Time!

- Serves 2
- A Little Effort / Vegan Option / Gluten-Free Option
- Wok to wonderful in 30 minutes
- Hero ingredient: turmeric (page 21)

Bánh Xèo Vegetable & Noodle Stuffed Sizzling Crêpe

Ooh La La, Ho Chi Minh

Yeah, we know the French are the crêpe Kings. But bánh xèo gives them a run for their money. You'll find these gorgeous little pancakes in any good food market these days. Originally from Ho Chi Minh, they're stuffed with greens and herbs, and slathered in the delicious nước chấm style dipping sauce. The ultimate Vietnamese street food, even if their roots are a little ooh la la.

30g (1oz) dried rice vermicelli noodles
vegetable oil, for frying the crêpes
lime wedges, to serve

FOR THE BATTER:
2 level tablespoons rice flour
100ml (3½fl oz) coconut milk
75ml (2½fl oz) cold water
¼ teaspoon ground turmeric
1 teaspoon cornflour (corn starch) or potato starch
small pinch of sea salt

FOR THE DIPPING SAUCE:
1 tablespoon rice vinegar
1 tablespoon honey (or use agave syrup for a vegan alternative)
½ tablespoon Mr Lee's Healthy Mussel Sauce (page 24), or ready-made fish sauce (or use Mr Lee's Vegan 'Fish' Sauce, page 25, for a vegan alternative)
½ teaspoon garlic paste, or 1 garlic clove, crushed and finely chopped
½ large fresh red chilli finely chopped
1 teaspoon freshly chopped coriander (cilantro) stems
½ tablespoon lime juice

FOR THE FILLING:
25g (1oz) bean sprouts
40g (1½oz) iceberg or romaine lettuce, finely shredded
handful of fresh herbs, like mint, coriander (cilantro), Thai basil, etc.
200g (7oz) your choice of cooked seafood, meat and/or tofu

Place the noodles in a bowl of freshly boiled water and leave to soak for 5 minutes. Drain and set aside.

Make the crêpe batter by mixing all the ingredients together in a mixing bowl, then set aside.

Next, mix together all the dipping sauce ingredients in a small bowl and set aside.

Take the filling ingredients and divide each into roughly 8 evenly sized portions.

Heat 1 teaspoon vegetable oil in a large frying pan (skillet) over a medium heat. Gently drop 1½ tablespoons of the crêpe mixture into the pan and swirl around the pan to form a pancake. You can use the back of a big spoon or spatula to do this, making gentle circles, starting from the centre.

When the crêpe sets and starts colouring up a bit, carefully flip it. Now place a portion of the bean sprouts, lettuce and herbs on the crêpe, followed by a portion of the seafood, meat and/or tofu. Cook for another 30 seconds, and then carefully fold the crêpe in half. Transfer the crêpe on to a serving plate and repeat the same process to make the remaining crêpes. Serve the crepes with the dipping sauce on the side, plus some lime wedges, if you like.

Vietnamese Celebration Wraps with Fresh Crab & Scallop

Wrapper's Delight

You'll find these little beauties at big celebrations, usually surrounded by a throng of hungry diners. In Vietnam, they use pork, but we've ditched the pig for juicy, vitamin-rich seafood. It's the perfect party food and goes with everything. If you can't find the little noodle cakes, you can try lettuce wrapped rice noodles. Party on, noodles!

8 fine vermicelli noodle cakes, or use 90g (3¼oz) dried rice noodles (plus 8 Little Gem lettuce leaf cups, to use as wrapper for loose noodles)
90g (3¼oz) large king or queen scallops
½ teaspoon vegetable oil
pinch of sea salt and freshly ground pepper

FOR THE DRESSING:
½ tablespoon Mr Lee's Healthy Mussel Sauce (page 24) or ready-made fish sauce
1 generous teaspoon honey or agave syrup
¼ lemongrass stalk, finely chopped, or ¼ teaspoon ground dried lemongrass
½ tablespoon rice vinegar
¼ large red chilli, finely chopped
¼ green chilli, finely chopped
¼ teaspoon lime zest
½ tablespoon lime juice

TO SERVE:
150g (5½oz) fresh or tinned crab meat, or use dressed crab
1½ tablespoons Mr Lee's Hoisin Sauce (page 25)
handful of baby spinach
handful of romaine or iceberg lettuce
small handful of fresh mint and Thai basil, or use European basil

In a small bowl , mix together all the dressing ingredients until well combined, then set aside.

Soak the noodle cakes, or rice noodles if using, in a bowl of freshly boiled water for 2–3 minutes, then drain and place on a serving dish.

Heat a frying pan (skillet) over a very high heat until smoking hot. While it's heating up, lightly brush the scallops with the vegetable oil. Once the pan is hot, add the scallops and cook on one side for 2 minutes, then flip over to cook for another minute on the other side. They should be just starting to turn golden brown. Place the cooked scallops on a serving plate and lightly season with the salt and pepper.

Serve the crab meat in a bowl or, if you're using dressed crab, serve the entire filled shell! Place the bowl with the dressing next to the serving plate, and place the hoi sin sauce in another small bowl next to it. Arrange the spinach and lettuce leaves in a bowl, and the rice noodle wraps on a platter (or loose noodles and lettuce leaves in a big bowl).

To make one, just lay a noodle cake on a plate or in your hand, add some lettuce, sauce, seafood toppings and a few torn herbs. Roll it up, give it another cheeky dip and you're good to go. If you're using loose noodles, use a bit of gem lettuce like a cup and fill it up with all that noodle goodness!

- Serves 4
- Showing Off / Gluten Free Option
- Wok to wonderful in 30 minutes
- Hero ingredients: salmon, spinach, lemongrass, coconut water and ginger (pages 21-22)

Mr Lee's Spicy Steamboat Hot Pot Noodles with Seafood & Greens

Alpine Asian Fondue Fusion (Try Saying That Ten Times)

Alpine fondue meets Asian attitude. Just like fondue, this hearty volcano of loveliness bubbles away while everyone gathers round, waiting to nab their favourite bits. Use whatever tender vegetables you like. In Vietnam they prefer water spinach, mustard greens or cabbage, as well as mushrooms like enoki or oyster. We've used prawns, but you can substitute with salmon, lean pork or beef.

FOR THE MARINATED MEAT OR FISH:
1 teaspoon Mr Lee's Healthy Mussel Sauce (page 24), or ready-made fish sauce
pinch of ground white pepper
½ teaspoon garlic paste, or use 1 garlic clove, crushed and chopped
150g (5½oz) raw king prawns (jumbo shrimp), or use salmon, beef or pork fillet

FOR THE BROTH:
6–8cm (2½–3¼in) piece of fresh root ginger, peeled and finely sliced, or substitute 2 tablespoons of ginger paste
2 lemongrass stalks, ends removed, crushed and finely chopped
2 tablespoons chilli paste, or use 2 whole fresh red chillies, finely chopped
300g (10½oz) brown crab meat
2 litres (3½ pints) boiling water
1 litre (1¾ pints) coconut water (100 per cent pure, no added sugar)

FOR THE DIPPING SAUCE:
2 tablespoons light soy sauce
½ tablespoon Mr Lee's Healthy Mussel Sauce (page 24), or ready-made fish sauce
½ teaspoon garlic paste, or 1 garlic glove, finely chopped
½ fresh or dried chilli, finely chopped

TO SERVE:
100g (3½oz) salmon fillet, cut into thin strips
200g (7oz) fresh clams, cleaned
300g (10½oz) spinach leaves
300g (10½oz) mustard green leaves, or chard or spring greens/cabbage
160g (5¾oz) dried rice vermicelli noodles, soaked in boiling water for 2 minutes, then drained

In a large bowl, mix together the fish sauce, garlic and white pepper. Add the meat or fish and mix it all up so it's nicely infusing. Leave to marinate for 20 minutes.

To make the broth, place a large saucepan over a high heat and add the ginger, lemongrass and chilli paste. Then add the brown crab meat, along with the boiling water. Simmer the broth for 3 minutes with the lid on, then strain it through a sieve and put the stock into a hot pot.

In a small bowl, mix the ingredients for the dipping sauce and set aside.

Finish off the broth by adding the coconut water, then place it over a portable gas stove in the middle of the table. You can also use a fondue stove, or any kind of hotpot with a little burner.

Arrange all the 'to serve' items on separate plates on the table, along with the dipping sauce and smaller bowls of noodles for each diner. Basically, you get stuck in and make your own bowl as you like it.

INDEX

THE NOODLE COOKBOOK

THE NOODLE COOKBOOK

Thanks

I guess the first person I should thank is you! I didn't think anyone read this bit. Whether it was intentional or accidental, you're here now. I'll try to make it worth it.

In 2014, I was diagnosed with stage 4 cancer, while trying to get a business off the ground and raise my boys; that's where my Mr. Lee's journey began. We're so time poor these days that often we settle for rubbish food because it's easy. This wasn't an option for me. I needed food that was fast, healthy and tasty that fitted with my life, work and health situation. No nasties or weird chemicals.

So much heart, soul and soy sauce has gone into making Mr. Lee's and this book. I'm incredibly proud of it and the people who've helped bring it to life.

Let's start with thanking my parents. Yes, we're going back that far, deal with it! Pull up a chair and let me take you back to Toorak, in Melbourne in the late 60's. Back then Oz wasn't the fusion food paradise it is now. Think British meat and two veg. That's when Kristine and Peter met at dad's Uni RMIT, fell in love and made me. My Dad was from Singapore, my mum's Australian; they LOVED food and how it brought people together. Once we moved onto Sydney in the 70's my parents were famous for their dinner parties. Exotic noodle dishes infused with the most delightful tongue-tingling spices and flavours. Everybody digging in together. Laughter, warmth and jokes that 10-year old me didn't get. My parents put me on this wonderful noodle journey and taught me that food should be fun. Thank you.

I want to thank my wife Weronika. Being married to a workaholic, serial entrepreneur dealing with cancer, but still spinning a million different projects, isn't as much fun as you might think. But Weronika makes it all work in my head. As she does in my life, she's made this book better in a million different ways. Thank you.

Every parent knows that children are the toughest food critics. If they don't like it, you'll know it. No sugar-coating, just straight-up and brutal. I want to thank my chief taste-testers, my sons James and Joshua. It took a while, but we won them over. You were tough but fair boys, thank you.

To Mr. Lee's co-founder, Graeme Hossie. A 'Get Shit Done' guy. I get to be the front man and do the interviews, but Graeme makes it happen. He's always had my back, believed in my crazy ideas and manages to always to fuel the hungry beast. No Graeme, No Mr. Lee's. Thank you, Graeme.

And to the whole Mr. Lee's crew bringing healthy, tasty noodle goodness to the world. When talented, committed people give you their energy to bring your vision to life. When your dream becomes their dream, it's humbling. Thank you.

Thanks to my personal noodle-Yoda, Andy Chu. Our Executive Chef who wrote the book on noodles. In this case, that's not a metaphor. There's a story and a history behind every dish. Andy knows them all. And you can taste that. It's deep and rich and real. Andy's our noodley heart. Thanks buddy, couldn't have done the book without you.

I want to thank Jackie Kearney, MasterChef supremo and all-round cooking legend. Jackie's brought her expertise, passion and love of all things noodle to our little book. James Roberts, my Creative chief who makes sure that this whole thing feels like Mr. Lee's. Martin Flavin, our copywriter who seems to have a limitless supply of noodle puns and a million different ways to say 'tastes nice'. Camilla and the Ebury crew at Penguin for keeping us on track, being patient, and sometimes being a badass when shit needed to get done. And our amazing photographers, Max and Liz Hamilton, and designer, Lucy Sykes-Thompson, who made this book look good enough to eat. Thank you.

I'm writing this in October 2020. We're just climbing our second COVID spike and a sneeze is now classified as a deadly weapon. It's been a pretty crappy year. I hope that by the time you read this, we'll have a vaccine and you'll be able to whip up a fat noodle feast for as many friends and family as you like. This year we clapped for healthcare workers, nurses and doctors. Selfless people who keep us alive. I've experienced this care, commitment and expertise first-hand throughout my treatment. Thanks doesn't feel like nearly enough.

Thank you for buying this book. I hope you discover a new ingredient, spice or flavour that you never knew existed. I hope you realise that your favourite dish might still be out there. I hope that on a rainy Wednesday evening, when you're just in the door and dog-tired, that this book helps you whip up some comforting, rejuvenating noodley goodness. I hope you get to have messy, fun, Kristine and Peter style dinner parties where you can wow your guests with your wok wizardry. May your pages be well thumbed, sticky and scorched. This book is for use, not display. I hope you use it so much it falls apart and then you have to go buy a new one.

Wishing you health, happiness and noodle goodness.
Damien aka Mr Lee

1

Published in 2021 by Ebury Press an imprint of Ebury Publishing,
20 Vauxhall Bridge Road,
London SW1V 2SA

Ebury Press is part of the Penguin Random House group of companies
whose addresses can be found at global.penguinrandomhouse.com

Text © Ebury Press 2021
Photography © Ebury Press 2021
Design © Studio Polka 2021

Photography: Haraala Hamilton
Food Styling: Jake Fenton
Prop Styling: Alexander Breeze
Recipe Writer: Jackie Kearney
Editor: Camilla Ackley

This edition first published by Ebury Press in 2021

www.penguin.co.uk

A CIP catalogue record for this book is available from the British Library

ISBN 9781529107463

Printed and bound in Latvia by Livonia Print SIA

Penguin Random House is committed to a sustainable future for our business, our readers and our planet.
This book is made from Forest Stewardship Council® certified paper.